The Cellar at the Top of the Stairs

Stephen Prasher was born in Lambeth,
South London, in 1959

Stephen Prasher

The Cellar
at the Top of
the Stairs

Pan Books London Sydney and Auckland

For Kate

First published in Great Britain 1988 by
William Heinemann Ltd

This edition published 1989 by Pan Books Ltd,
Cavaye Place, London SW10 9PG

9 8 7 6 5 4 3 2 1

© Stephen Prasher 1988

ISBN 0 330 30744 4

Photoset by Deltatype Ltd, Ellesmere Port
Printed and bound in Great Britain by
Cox & Wyman Ltd, Reading

Part One

1

'The problem is,' he said, 'that you don't know who's who.' He took a razor-blade out of his top pocket and made a series of precise chops at the sulphate. 'My friends, Nicola's friends, friends of friends, gatecrashers . . .' He licked his index finger and ran it into the corners of the mirror. 'People just passing. They hear the noise and come up.' He shrugged and swept the powder into a line four inches long, tapered at both ends. 'Want some?'

'I'd prefer a drink.'

'There's some beer in the fridge,' he said. 'I stashed some, or they would have drunk it all. Scavenging bastards.'

I kicked over a near-empty bottle on my way across the lounge. A trickle of wine dribbled on to the carpet and the bottle rocked and settled. The kitchen was full of the detritus parties like that always seem to leave behind them. It's as though really there's only one party and it goes round and round visiting the flats of people like Charlie; and it always leaves after it salad-stained paper plates and splintered plastic cups and cigarette burns – but never any cigarettes – and a prone body and empty cans and bottles and, of course, a slice of quiche face down on the floor. I stared at it and concluded that this one party – flying the night from flat to flat – must be a malicious-charactered sprite, throwing food and tantrums whenever people congregated. The party spirit. I side-stepped the splattered quiche and fumbled in the fridge for a beer.

3

Back in the lounge, Charlie had rolled a five-pound note into a tight tube and stuck it up his right nostril. He pressed down on his left nostril and dipped like a blue-beaked bird to the mirror. His eyes narrowed to thin points – very intense and very unfocused at the same time – then his straight, black hair curtained away his face. I watched the tube snuffling up the line. He paused midway. 'Do you remember much about last night?'

I didn't. I'd met an old friend on the way there and – although I thought we didn't have much to say to each other any more – we decided to make do. We were the best we could afford, in various senses. We settled for each other and decided to go to the pub first.

It suited us both. She said she hated arriving anywhere on time and I said that I hated arriving anywhere sober. So off we went with the express and very worthy intention of only downing two or three pints; but I had the unexpressed intention of drinking twice as fast as her and thus making damn sure that I got through a minimum of five.

Ethel (I regret to say it was her real name. Her father was an Anglican minister who probably thought that by so christening her he would deter suitors who weren't absolutely sincere in spirit) marked my pace and proceeded to match it. A long-distance drinker. Even when the landlord's bell had signalled the final lap she carried on keeping up with me. By this time I had begun quite to admire her. I'd also begun to suspect that turning up at the party only to collapse in an inebriated stupor might be deemed ill-mannered. So we shambled out of the pub like two old buildings about to be demolished, and I put my arm round her shoulder just to commemorate the ancientness of our friendship.

I smudgily recollected a pair of gratecrashers – brothers, possibly – timorously tacking in our wake, sidling behind us, black-suited, like Jehovah's Witnesses. And I remembered colliding with the front door of Charlie's flat and

4

discovering that it opened to my indelicate touch. There were some ragged cries of 'Eth! Angelo!' from a gaggle of satirists in the corridor. One of them added, with less kindness than justice, 'Pissed again.' I responded with an elegant 'Fuck off' and, having sounded what I considered to be the right note, parted the crowd with ungracious elbows and twitched myself like a divining rod towards the booze. Poor Eth. She was abandoned to the hugs and kisses of a harlequinade of resting actors. She did not emerge for some time.

I filled an inevitable plastic cup with an inevitable Yugoslavian wine. Down it went in one fell gulp: the arm's automatic assumption that it was still wielding beer. And the wine grazed the throat like gravel on the knee. Being a puritan at heart, and believing that all suffering works to one's moral betterment, I imposed the ordeal on myself again. It made me squint at the gathering with my favourite eye – the jaundiced one. All these familiar, unsuccessful faces, aspiring to things they would never attain. I congratulated myself that no one was talking to me.

A flat cocktail of partyness – that's what I was looking at. Something slung together out of obvious ingredients that just didn't work. Part of the problem was that there was more cock than tail. The sex-market losers sniffed caninely about, despairing of some crumb of fuckability. The temporary couples slavered prettily, wishing that they could bite success that minute. Two different modes of frustration, I mused forensically.

No; I hadn't forgotten how misanthropic I was; but I couldn't remember anything to the point. I had talked to Nicola – Charlie's live-in girlfriend and provider of ready cash – about her latest money-making scheme. (These schemes of hers were rather like the Yeti: much spoken of by her more excitable acquaintances, but never conclusively sighted.) She had stood toe-tip to toe-tip with me, her vinous breath gusting into my face, and whispered:

'I've cracked it.'

'Ah,' I said. An alien elbow pried hard into my liver.

'The big one. A dating agency for the unemployed.' She paused, breath held, waiting for my wonderment.

'Ah,' I repeated. 'Many takers?'

'Not yet,' she admitted. Then, 'We've only just started. They're all out there, you know. Millions of them. Don't laugh.'

She was too late, though; I'd already begun. I was assailed by one of my frequent visions, an imagining of the ridiculous and the squalid: those workless numbers knotting, the baked bean tins rattling in the cupboard, more little burdens for the welfare state; and Nicola's chubby hands filled with the goodies from ten thousand dole cheques. And then I stopped. I had remembered I was unemployed. For the moment. At present. Now.

I pointed to an unfamiliar figure – a man scruffy enough to be either a tramp or a computer programmer. He was listening to Charlie, frowning, as though at a joke he didn't understand. His black hair was plastered flat down almost to his eyebrows and one leg was so badly twisted at the kneecap that he appeared to be standing on a slope.

'There,' I said. 'A likely customer.'

And Nicola had bounced away – her blue and yellow striped jeans stretched tight across her bum – offended, I believe, to spread the creed of capitalism elsewhere.

I had fervently wished that whoever was smoking dope would stop. It had swum through my brain like a great, brown fish, its turbulent fins swishing. I had suffered the music as it resolved itself to a single, dead drum. However much I drank my throat became drier as if, in fact, the wine was drinking me. And there had been a fracas – something like a fight but less terminal. Arms and legs signalling unsober distress. And Eth. I must record Eth, who loomed out of the night and said:

'I suppose you think we ought to sleep together.'

'It would be the companionable thing to do,' I replied.

'But – ' she said.

'But – ' I said. And we left it at that.

6

Resigned to my incapacity, I settled down on an enormous turquoise bean-bag to snooze superficially through early and late morning, turning obligingly to avoid a clodhopping dancer as and when expediency dictated.

So I felt it was only honest to say to Charlie that, no, I didn't recall anything relevant.

'See?' he said. 'We've no way of finding out.'

'What are you going to do then?' I asked. 'You can't just leave it there.'

Charlie always had to be pushed. He needed a certain amount of pressure applied to him if he was to do anything. Admittedly, there were some matters he regularly managed by himself – like setting up a deal or playing a video game with casual, interminable co-ordination. But, generally, a constant force applied from the rear was the only way to get him moving.

'It'll work itself out,' he announced. He was a great believer in providence. It was as though he lived his whole life in a restaurant, confident that the eternal waiter would remove his problematic plate.

I looked at him and wondered if he would continue that way for ever. He wasn't doing badly so far. The sun was slanting in flat slabs through his windows. The serviceable, leaf-green faded furniture rested, untouched by whatever had been committed on it the night before. Nicola was out working behind a bar. A bottle of Valium was balanced on one arm of the chair and a sachet of speed on the other. The Sunday lunchtime world hummed in tune with his gentle metabolism.

'You'll have to call the police,' I suggested blasphemously.

Charlie gestured lazily to the floor. At his feet was the mirror with its razor-blade and its white-flecked surface. Roaches lay scattered over the floor like stones in a field. A V-folded boat of silver paper, singed underneath, rocked from keel to keel with the breeze slipping under the door. In truth, an incriminating landscape.

7

'God knows where it all is,' he said. 'I don't. They'd want to talk to everyone. Me. You. For hours and hours. In square rooms. Suspicious-minded buggers.'

I took a long swig of beer. The can bit acidly on my lips and I listened to the lager somersault fizzingly down to my stomach. The difficulty I was facing was how to make Charlie appreciate the intractability of what had happened. Mentally, he acknowledged that there was a problem to be disposed of; but this didn't stop him from doing nothing about it. And, shuddering in the shadow of a pile of alcohol, I was in no mood to be energetic myself. For the sake of making something happen, though, I tried to sound urgent:

'Come and look at it.' My voice reached out firmly, like a hand trying to wrest him from repose.

'I know it's there,' he said. 'I know what it looks like.' He grinned as if he'd thought of something very clever. 'Would you like some tomato soup?'

He began a giggle. It started quietly, with spaces between each ripple, like one that was making up its mind whether or not to possess his mouth. Then it ran out uninterruptedly, bubbling over his teeth. His palms spread out to accept his spasmed face.

My little, sudden surge of effort had passed him by or induced a shocking result. A current misdirected.

2

I didn't see Charlie for a day or two. To put it another way, I couldn't afford to see him or anyone else. I'd spent almost all my money with Eth on pre-party measures when I could have got drunk there for free. So, on Sunday evening, I bought forty cigarettes, a loaf of bread and – to supply those life-sustaining, ever-necessary vitamins – a jar of Marmite. Then I set myself to wait for Thursday morning's post.

Waiting and being ill are the two conditions that make me think. Waiting in a grey-brown, lightless room intensifies the necessity. Nothing to stare at but a red-rimmed poster of Debbie Harry. I kept the curtains drawn so I wouldn't have to see people going to the pub, anticipating great cylinders of amber beer. Sitting in my seasonal, adjustable, inappropriate deckchair I watched my mind turning like a worm on the carpet. A dry, muddy trace, twisting.

My thoughts kept returning to what I had seen on the mattress. It had been battered until it curled, self-protectingly, into the posture of a foetus. There had been petals of blood scattered around it and these, I guessed, no bed of roses either. I shivered and imagined the fists and feet bludgeoning at her body, and the body being jolted up and down, forward and back, with that gasping gug-gug-gug sound coming out; until she surrendered her teeth like a necklace on a scarlet thread; until she surrendered everything.

It was a bruise on the mind, something felt distantly. It didn't quite belong to me; like luggage lying at a foreign airport.

I tried to give the body a history. Unknown, uninhabited, I tried to breathe life into it. To produce it backwards. To redeem it, even, in the past; with my arm breaking the pool, reaching for something refracted in the water, hoping that. . .

She was happy and she was going to a party, pink in the pink bathroom. Her forearm squeaked against the mirror as she cleared a circle beyond the steam. Then she could look at herself. She could decide to be satisfied with herself and to acquaint herself with this being enough. She knew why she used to be called apple blossom, why she used to be told that she was pretty as a picture. She suspected that those were the fair average of the compliments she would continue to receive – for the next few years at least. Because she knew that those were compliments suitable for girls and that she would be measured for others when she was older.

I didn't want to see her more clearly than that yet. I didn't want to see more than her bath-flushed face. I certainly didn't want to observe the mechanics of dressing. I kept her obscured by condensing steam, allowing myself merely to watch the long, exact moment when – head still and eye pinned motionless to its own reflection – she drew back a lash-feathered lid and underlined it with a coal-blue curve.

She must have done that at the dressing-table in her bedroom. I had deduced that she was someone who would have wanted to do things properly. I gave her to think, 'Now I shall do my make-up,' and to sit down, square to the mirror, and to do it. I decided that she had a respect for going out – a conception of it as something positively to be done and not as something casually to be slipped into. She was not, I concluded, familiar with the iterative party and its spite. She was going to visit it with that eagerness for the new friend who will shortly become a bore; the first one to offer friendship in an alien place.

Who had invited her, I wondered. I had already assumed too much of her innocence to believe that she was a gatecrasher, or even that she had the courage to accept a third-hand invitation. A second-hand invitation, perhaps. A more experienced woman – someone at work, concerned by young loneliness – saying, 'Come along on Saturday night. Meet a few people.' And she had protested that she couldn't, that she didn't know anyone. 'But that's the point. Get to know them.' And she protested again, shyly, prepared to concede because she didn't want always to be shy. And 'No,' said the more experienced woman – clattering pen and provisional lipsticks into her handbag, tidying the desk, preparing to leave the office – 'It'll be all right. We can go for a drink first.' The promise of introductions and the hint of protection.

She finished her make-up in her fluffy bedroom. I was sure it was a fluffy bedroom, full of soft, stuffed toys. Not saved from childhood. Not dragged out of childhood, memories adhering to them like chewing gum. Not a propped, lumpy teddy bear, for example; adhering to it an image of itself hurled with hatred behind a sofa – rejected for the sake of those who gave it; or clasped as the only one worth loving in the face of those who gave it. Not that. The fluffiness I felt was new, acquired for this bedroom, furnishing it like a pristine childhood. Amiable, creamy monsters shaken on to the pillows like powder; a tea-cosy cat, perpetually about to purr; five furry, unarmed aliens, suspended like planets from the ceiling.

I decided that she must have had a duvet – a pastel rectangle, in pale blue. Given that this was a rented flat, given that I knew that she had moved to London only recently, I could assume that the carpet, the wallpaper, the chair by the bed and the dressing-table itself were not of her choosing. They were discountable. They told me nothing about her.

But, on imagining them more closely, I realised that, indirectly, they whispered. The landlady who had chosen them. The landlady she had chosen. Two sets of expectations tightening up on each other, like turning a lid on a jar. Enclosing this material life. She may not have sought deliberately the maternal, spherical, commercial figure who answered her enquiries. The landlady who had trodden sedately from what she still called the parlour, preparing to present her no-nonsense aspect, believing that once finance and regulations had been set out unambiguously, pastoral encompassment could begin. The landlady, who had never had children herself but had learnt that, in this big city, a shoulder of lamb and a shoulder to cry on were often needed comforts for a girl far from home. The landlady, I noticed, who had furnished the room to let using as her model the cold, winter guest-rooms where she had Christmassed with Edwardian aunts and uncles.

And she – the girl – stepped out from that last Saturday evening. Her shoes tapped down the staircase. Fingers on a piano running over two octaves, accelerating into light-ness. For the first time I glimpsed the back of her head as she detoured to the parlour door – having adopted the word out of embarrassed politeness at its anachronism – and sang, 'I may be late back tonight. Don't wait up.' Her head slanted to the left as she lilted out the litany. Short brown hair, tucking up beneath itself just before it ended, swinging vertical. Right ear's ghost-pale rim behind the shaken strands.

And she stepped out into the street. Redundant chimneys glowed clay-orange against the unpatched sky. There were not many people about because it was early evening. But she was nervous, excited, inventing all the people she would like to meet. Besides, she had her rendezvous with her new friend to keep. Someone with social engagements and a schedule. Not this expansive time of singleness – I thought she would have thought.

I didn't know then her exact destination. I followed her as far as I could, but, when she turned to go to the tube station, I watched her and let her go. Her hair spread slightly out and then subsided as the rhythm of each downward step played against the upward air. Trying out her wings.

I had seen her off, for the time being. But I was intent on finding her again, recovering her, asking her how she came to be dead. I had not yet constructed a narrative commen-surate with her fate. It wasn't that I expected the beginning to weigh equally with the conclusion. That bludgeoned finale, that blackjack on the skull-less brain, I never wanted to dream for myself an inaugurating blow like that. This beginning, though – this silly, happy beginning, this comic worm performing on the carpet – it hadn't even the premonition of that end. Nothing in it prefiguring the broken body calling through indifferent noise for help; nothing prefiguring a supplicant's crawl stopped with a grab at the ankle. The door so near. The door so far. And closed.

I imagined that when my dole cheque came I would go looking. Disturb Charlie. Steal his drugs and withdraw him into talk. Question Nicola. Demand the identity of the mysterious older woman. Deliver a Bogartian slap. Search, search, search. Stop drinking and keep my wits about me. Buy a hat. Connect the beginning to the end. The strands of truth reach to the highest knitting-machines. Practise the turned-up collar and the hatchet face. A face to open doors with.

The landlady, too. Patting back her grey, night-netted hair she blinked into the hall on Sunday morning. Tightened her lips at the light burning into daytime. Considered this curiosity as she bent to gather up her *Mail on Sunday*. She read it tetchily, tipping tea from pot to cup without looking up. No girl emerged for breakfast. Nor from her room at all. A discreet, inch-ajar investigation confirmed the worst: she had not come home last night. The landlady had worried through the day. And the next. Days spent in shuffling ornaments millimetres to left or right, backwards or forwards.

Find her and tell her, I resolved. End the worry running through her rearranging habits like a scab. And I perceived instinctively that with a woman like that – whose principles were as straight and indigestible as bamboo – the fact of unattributable, unavenged murder would pierce through her like a hat-pin to the heart; resulting in a cold, pained Fury, driven by robbery to revenge. My grandmotherly partner, sweetly avoiding the police. In the evenings, we would discuss the day's discoveries over rashers and eggs and fried toast.

I creaked my back forward from the deckchair's wooden frame, like a bow that had been bent too long by an archer's

13

patient hands. Between my knees a stale-crumbed plate and a tangential, Marmite-smeared knife came into view.

It was Tuesday night and I had ten cigarettes left. Not counting the one I was assiduously smoking. Outside, I could hear loose change burbling as it strode to the pub. I looked at my watch and prayed that soon, with a little more thinking, I would be tired enough to sleep. Until the next hungry, thought-fraught day.

In the early hours – the nothing time adrift between dark and dawn – my mind shouts schemes into the stillness, and the echoes return even bigger. Or I dream Byzantine plots, play chess in three dimensions, untangle serpentine conundrums; and by five a.m. my room is full of ambitions, shadows rubbing shoulders, each urging the others to be real.

Then morning comes and sends them all away. (I don't know where they go to; perhaps Australia.) Morning without postmen. I still listened for the postman; the snap-bang letterbox and the paper swish on the horsehair mat, the letter like a brush on a hushed drum – concentrating for that tiny sibilance to usher out the huge silliness of last night.

For a long time I listened with my eyes shut. There was no point in opening them because I knew what they would see if I did. The sea-green ceiling with its triangular, untenanted cobweb. The reversed pattern of thin, printed curtains, through which light leaked like brine into a rotten boat. A shambled stack of newspapers, representing the first Thursdays, Fridays and Saturdays of fortnights marked out by raindropping dole cheques. From the last eight months, dammit. A tragically unused ashtray, cumbersomely pocketed one closing time.

And books – I had dozens I could have read. I'd bought them, I imagine, during the years of plenty when I thought nothing – practically nothing – of spending up to five pounds at a time. (The years, incidentally, when I was employed intermittently as an actor; travelling in transit

14

vans to theatres which, like a progression of Chinese boxes, grew successively smaller; not so much alienating audiences as merely boring them, and finally boring even myself to the point where I precipitately closed this parenthetical episode in my existence.) But I couldn't look at these fictions any longer. On every page some tantalising, silver-handed demon was offering a drink to his companion. Characters refuelling themselves as often as big cars. In books even the Irish could afford to drink. Apparently.

And the many ways to spend the day. Go for a walk; risk being in the world outside and not allowed to touch it. The whole world as a shopping arcade denied to me. Sit in the deckchair; its hard, wooden line across my neck. And think. Stay in bed and think. Think about the girl. With regard to whose existence I was, this morning, sceptical. The littleness of another day's commencement.

The memory of what I had seen had shrunk and become, somehow, artificial. It was as though I saw myself moving through Charlie's flat with a puppet's stilted slowness, contained on a miniature stage. I recollected myself getting up from the turquoise bean-bag, leaving the concave imprint of my head, back and legs behind me. It was six a.m., imprecisely. I considered the possibility that the back room – occupied usually by non-functional electrical appliances, a bike and a mattress – might at this hour be copulation free. The corridor down which I zigzaggingly staggered was deserted, except for a scarlet shoe – its attenuated heel snapped like the step from a glass. An unsteady Terpsichorean female left fifty per cent flat-footed. I watched my inexplicable, vandalistic kicking of the shoe. It thumped on to the lavatory door, from which issued a low, vomitory groan.

I watched myself thumping in person at another door – the one to the back room. It was jammed. My left hand twisted and shoved the handle. My right pressed at the top whilst my foot jarred at the bottom, where the obstruction was. I assumed it was the bike – toppled in some intimate jollity. And I set about the door with rigour, vigour and a modicum of violence; the co-ordination of shoulder and thigh, charging a full yard at full speed from the opposite wall, like a rugby player about to dip over the try line and score. I remembered that before the moment of triumph there was an unfamiliar sound – an indeterminate, brief grinding succeeded by a flop. I stopped to test my powers of recognition. My solitary party game when everyone else had fucked off – identify the mystery sound. The best I could come up with was some damage to the bike, probably requiring repair and apologies. Or a clockwork frog bellying off a log. It was time to open the door.

I broke off this observation of myself. What I couldn't avoid seeing next I had already transformed into a black and white photograph. I had dredged it through some mental tray and it had come out looking like a picture belonging to a pathologist's report or a courtroom drama. Holding it by the corners as it dripped off its last chemical beads, I presented it to my memory again. Inescapably the same this morning as it was that. She was lying on her side. Her left forearm was bent up across her eyes, her elbow pressed into the mattress. Her right arm had been forced impossibly back behind her head. At an angle, I had thought, like a gallows; as though she were hanging herself. And then the realisation swelled up slowly through me that its curious position had been caused by my assault on the door; that the arm had been locked in a gesture of survival – like a swimmer's striking for a shore – until I had snapped it backward in its socket.

She was real enough – but I dismissed her from my mind. I had no wish to inflict too much vividness on myself. Besides, I had begun to suspect that Charlie had been playing a joke on me. The corpse – that had been there all right; it was somehow the circumstances surrounding it that were wrong.

Charlie had been complacent. He had laughed. He had

16

singularly failed to be alarmed. It was impossible not to believe that he had some secret, simple scheme for clearing the matter up. Perhaps he was merely waiting for Nicola to return. Perhaps he had been amused at my perplexity. Perhaps, perhaps, perhaps. Whatever it was, I was sure that basically, mysteriously, it had been resolved by now.

Anyway, there was always Nicola. In spite of her predilection for absurd schemes – her tendency, almost, to be gulled by herself – she had a nervous instinct for her own preservation. She shied away from trouble like a lamb from an electric fence. I well remembered how, at the end of the great cheque card scam, she had strolled out of Selfridges seconds before the police had tumbled in. She turned only once to watch their Keystone entrance; and afterwards she had explained that she had simply known; that she was getting 'bad vibes'. So I was sure that she would have extricated both of them; would have tidied up – her pink arms flurrying as Charlie sat serene – and rung the guardians of the law; who would have told her – in the time-honoured but indispensable phrase – not to touch anything. And they would have arrived in due course with their cars and an ambulance and, yes, I was convinced of it, everything would have happened as it should have.

In short, my speculations were prepared to hand the whole matter over to the authorities. A plastic sheet. The trolley to the fridge. Official channels drawing on their official explanations. Inquests and trials, if they liked, as long as they didn't involve me. Consign the lot of it to those who knew best. Give my imagination a rest, along with those other parts of me currently doing bugger all.

I lit a cigarette in celebration of this sudden cessation of thought. It was the limit of what I could allow myself in these reduced conditions. I resolved that I would soon have breakfast, feasting on black coffee and Marmite. The comestible equivalent of sackcloth and ashes. In penitence for my poverty. And I had exorcised that infestation of my mind; replaced it with an empty head, ready to be filled up again.

3

I had just resolved to spend the day imagining being rich – strolling the gardens of infinite cash, where champagne bottles grew like pineapples between spiky leaves – when the doorbell rang. Panic. A quick run through the list of creditors. A very short list, if only because it was so difficult to get credit; but long enough, in these days of impossibility. Be bold, I said to myself. Be resolute. Be brazen. My heart banged from side to side, like a pendulum between two possibilities. Tell the truth: I have no money, kind sir. Dearly though I would love to oblige you, I cannot do so at this moment. In time. Lie: I shall soon have the requisite funds, upon which instant all reasonable demands will be met. Assuredly. Oscillating, in fact, between two different sorts of lie.

A shape resolute at the bell once again. Someone indecipherable through the opaque glass; a face moving and breaking across its distortions. I opened the door breathlessly, having faith in inspiration and the value of assessing a situation on its own merits.

'Charles! My son!'

'Angelo, my child.'

'What's the time?'

'Pub time,' he said. 'Half-past eleven.'

Much later than I thought. My soft service, my hissing postal alarm, had failed me. I smiled foolishly, like a priest being invited to an orgy. 'No money. It's a chronic disability.'

'I come bearing good gifts,' said Charlie.

'*Timeo Charlies et dona ferentes,*' I replied. I was being honest. Charlie was a drugs man and I, I suppose, I was in favour of keeping the throat damp. To excess I didn't like dry consumption. I didn't want to find myself set up in his arid landscape, pursuing a contact from one pub to another. Pints interrupting like hyphens along the way. An unsatisfying, unsettling pursuit.

'Uh uh,' he grunted. 'This one's easy. Fifty for doing nothing. For what you've already done.' He waved five brown flags at me. A signal for surrender.

'Explain,' I bargained.

'When we're in the pub,' said Charlie. 'Take it.'

'Let me get my coat.' As quick as that. The sight of money and the prospect of a pint. A hand offering and a hand taking. Need asks few questions. The transaction complete. For the first time in weeks I was wealthy.

We walked to the pub. A distance that could be covered in less than two minutes, provided one strode out briskly. Which I did. Charlie on half-sail behind me, moving with the grace of a ship upon the restless waves. And in. As though to a harbour where no winds blew. 'Two pints of bitter please.'

The landlady stumped along the bar to the taps, greasy finger and greasy thumb pincering the glasses. I deduced that she had been margarining the lunchtime sandwiches, stacked in their perspex box. A wet slice of ham poked out at me like a tongue: dead pig processed into slimy strips. The disgustingness of food, compared with this wholesome thirst flushing up from my stomach to my throat. Pearls of sweat strung across my forehead. Jewellery, perforce, for this celebration, as the flushing rose through me again. My hands ticking too as I endured the time it took the slothful old witch to pour. Peel off some paper and a long swig before we sit.

We sat down. The table tilted with the weight of my elbows and two shallow pools of orange beer slopped towards them, a grey rim of foam popping on each perimeter. Soaking through my shirt. No matter. I would drink till I was dry.

'What's it all about?' I asked.

'Alas,' said Charlie, 'I saw the answer last night, figured in a circle on the carpet; but I returned this morning and, though the carpet was still there, the answer had gone – vanished – departed.' He spread his hands upwards, as though releasing a dove.

'But, more specifically,' I clarified, 'this'.

'Ah,' said Charlie. 'Have another drink.'

'Sure. Your pleasure.' Not one to refuse, although I guessed I was being softened up; made soggy, in fact, like bread soaked in water. Must remember not to crumble into saturated bits of me.

Cling to this red-gold pub, I enjoined myself. Where the wallpaper ascended maroon and furry to the Victorian cornice and the stuccoed ceiling writhed with heavy mouldings. The shapes of ugly, pointed flowers; grotesque flowers too symetrically complex ever to have existed. Elaboration wound over elaboration for the sake of elaboration. Old money invested in old excess. And, from a different time – the cheap time of now – these vinyl-covered seats. Bum-sliding vinyl melted into blotches by fag ends. From baroque to utility. An economic parable, I mused.

And Charlie returned from the bar. Settling into this session with an enthusiasm that mimicked mine. The quiet comfort of the professional drinker. Not like him at all. Usually it was minuscule mouthfuls and his nerves edging him away somewhere quieter. For a smoke, or similar. This dissembling, therefore, indicated that something was afoot. A mystery smuggled into the caverns of his mind. I told myself that it would be prudent to avert my eyes, to refuse to know anything of the clandestine baggage transported in the course of his dealings. Poor but honest me.

'The money. You said it was for doing nothing.'

'Mmn.' He sipped and nodded at the same time. Pushing away from questions like a punter with his pole, a river-bed of asking remaining still beneath him. I thought I detected his hand squeezing his glass. Further delay while he lit a cigarette. I glanced at his barometric eyes. Their black pupils seemed to recede in on themselves, as though I were looking at them through an extending zoom lens – a measure of the pressure he was under, forcing his way to an answer. A cloud of smoke swirling in his open mouth, equilibrially poised between escape and capture, before it was sucked down. Speech. 'I had a visitor just after you left. On Sunday. He made me an offer.'

'Which you couldn't refuse.' A smear of unjustifiable sarcasm. Charlie always presented his transactions as favours, helping those who couldn't help themselves; to the goodies.

'You should be grateful to me,' he insisted with an air of injured philanthropy. 'I had your best interests at heart, my son. You never have any money. You don't invest wisely.'

'The brewing industry. What could be more vital to the nation's health?'

'Corpses,' he said. 'Everybody needs corpses.'

I assumed this was the cue for a procrastinating pun and tried to pre-empt the punchline. Nothing doing. 'Go on.'

'There's a thriving trade in death. The world's full of corpses, and nobody's thought of selling them before. But I have. I sold the girl. Or her body.'

Me searching through those words like a man waking up in the dark looking for his spectacles, hand bumping on the bedside table, sure they are there somewhere. The man alarmed, needing his sharper sight. And me convinced that there had to be sense stuffed somewhere in what Charlie had said; but, either through mishearing or misinterpretation, unable to find it. Reshuffling the words and discovering nothing. Conceding that what I'd heard he must have said. Then the words having the effect of extreme hunger. An expanded emptiness, as though I had been floated into a celestial dimension where the physical appearances of this solid world were only distantly graspable. Rules suspended to clear the air for insanity. Let the game begin. My brain stretching like a balloon to encompass this enormity.

'Fuck me,' I muttered. 'You can't do that.'

It appeared that he had done it. It appeared that the happening had happened. No matter how much I questioned Charlie it stayed insistently there. Immovable. A fact carved in stone. With the creaking patience of a hod carrier's back, I tried to shift it. Bruised my fists and scraped away their translucent skin, petulant that anything could so stubbornly exist. But the fact had emerged and the fact remained. Like this:

A man, said Charlie, had come to the door. He was in his late fifties and he behaved like a general – like someone who had an invisible army with him, ready to do his bidding. His hair was shorn back very short, as if he hated the sight or thought of it; any shorter, apparently, and it would have been down to the skin and the skull. His torso was like a table and his head like a smaller table set on top of it, with no neck intervening.

'He sounds,' I suggested, 'like a sort of executive skinhead.'

But for once Charlie didn't respond to my little joke. He seemed almost entranced by this figure, in the same way as people are gripped by the inexplicable logic of their own nightmares. He went on describing him.

He had the stiff, thick legs of an idol and he wore blunt, black shoes. His eyes were slate-grey and he had stared at everything and been surprised by nothing. His hands had swung heavily by his hips.

And I could imagine him now. I placed him in a jungle (why? because I knew intuitively that he was not merely lawless but beyond the bounds of civilisation) stepping slowly between the trees, the creepers tearing, the parrots shrieking overhead. He was made of stone – an animated statue; his face sheer as a cliff.

'And,' added Charlie lightly – relapsing, suddenly relaxing – 'he smoked a fat, brown cigar. A turd between his teeth.'

We both laughed like men dismissing a ghost.

'So,' I asked, 'what happened next?'

The man had said, 'I hear you have a corpse for sale. Let me see it.'

'I told him to come in,' Charlie went on. 'I'd been worried about that corpse. More worried than you thought I was. I'd made up my mind that the only thing I could do was to wait until Nicola got back. Then we could have tidied up and called the police.' He sat there with his hands in his pockets and his legs stretched out straight in front of him. Looking like a tennis player between sets, getting thrashed and not even understanding why. 'But if this man knew already. If all he wanted was the body . . .' He picked up a beer mat and tapped its edge on the rim of his glass. Recollecting his own reasons. And under what circumstances he had them. 'Besides,' – a decisive tap – 'I didn't want to have to tidy up.'

'Problem solved,' I remarked. 'Didn't you feel there was a moral dimension here? Don't you think it's a trifle exploitative? Selling a murdered girl for a few shillings?'

'No worse than exploiting the living. Which, you assure me, goes on all the time.'

'It's fucking outrageous,' I told him, overlooking the slur on my neglected socialism.

'You didn't have to take the money.'

'I didn't know what it was for.'

'You do now,' said Charlie. 'It's blood money. For a few stone of dead person. Flesh and blood money. Do you want to give it back? I'll make sure it gets to your favourite charity.'

Right at that moment I wished I could have thrown down

23

his fifty pounds and left and gone to another pub; made my grand gesture of refusal before I got contaminated. Out of the question, though – if only because I'd already started spending it. I was finding the experience guiltily congenial, as if I were drinking from another man's well. 'On with the story,' I concurred. 'Morally unmolested.'

The man had walked down the hall with a rock's slow, avalanchine, forward stumble. The light coming from behind him. His arms curved unwieldy beside him. As though he used them to bracket himself off. In black parentheses. 'Where is it?' he had demanded.

'How much?' Charlie confused, bemused, perturbed, but trying to salvage something from the situation; like trying to pluck an object from a dream, clutch it till wakebreak, as proof that the dream was dreamt.

'One hundred. No more,' the man had said.

'He wasn't the sort of person you could negotiate with,' Charlie explained. 'In a way, he was doing me a favour. And he might have just taken it. I wouldn't have been able to stop him. He would have swatted me like Frankenstein's monster.' Image of a steel-plated arm's lethargic, monstrous sweep. Charlie's mortal thinness gasping against the wall. 'So I led him to the back room. The hinges on the door had been sprained and I could see her right arm.' A different arm from the one that I'd imagined; not the icing-cake arm beloved from Quasimodo to King Kòng. 'It had been driven back into the shoulder socket. Jutted out like a broken spoke from a bicycle wheel.'

The man had gone in. The solitary god in that cluttered shrine. 'Surveying the merchandise, I suppose,' Charlie said. 'In such cases *caveat emptor*, no doubt.' He drifted into silence. Discovering the misery of it all as cynicism lapped over cynicism. The misery of this dirty sale. Necessary, convenient, forced on him. 'He took it. Came out of the room, said, "It'll do," counted out the money. Scooped the body up. As if it were a sack of potatoes and he was afraid of losing one. And he carried it off.

'I watched him cross the street from the lounge window. Lumbering along with the conscience of a caveman. The passers-by must have assumed it was his wife or something. Paralytic. He had an estate car.'

'Perhaps purchased for exactly that sort of cargo.' I was trying to lighten his spirits, but it was my second witticism to fall fractionally flat.

'Perhaps.'

'And nothing more?'

'Nothing more.' Levelling them out. Two weary words. 'I felt relieved when she'd gone. A guest who had overstayed.'

4

Eth raging at me. Her red hair tempestuous around her face and her face white like the moon in stormy skies. Cloud-strands blowing across it. Less placid than the cold, impassive moon, though, regarding our peccadilloes. 'How could you!' she screamed. Bent forward over me, hands clutching upwards as if trying to grasp my intangible stupidity. Emerald fingernails. Very Italianate when she was angry, our Eth.

'I didn't do anything.' Lying face up on my bed. Staring at the ceiling. At the cobweb, deserted by an upwardly mobile spider. Trying to count the sagging and severed wisps. Always the last pint that did the damage.

'If it had been a man it would have been different. Call the police! Notify the press! Fascist conspirators strike against the left! But since it was only a girl,' sarcasm as delicate in the mouth as curdled cream, 'since it was only a girl, sell her for beer money.'

'Unfair. I bought some cigarettes.'

'You bought some cigarettes! That makes it all right?' Shoe stabbed at mattress. Futile. This lumpish mattress as unrufflable as a rhino. 'Do you know what you are? You're a typical bloody man.'

'That hurts, Eth. That really hurts.'

'And you're drunk. Otherwise you'd be taking this more seriously. I'm going to make you talk to me. I'm going to make you swallow a cup of tea. Any tea in this slum?'

My arm signposting the kitchen – like all signposts, only approximate. Eth's feet announcing that her anger had not abated. A rude inruption on my supine siesta, showing no prospect of sodding off. This time of day was much respected in the colonies. I shut my eyes and pictured banana groves leading down to a beach bar, and beyond that the sea. The grey-black sea, rotating vastly as one slow whirlpool. Sucking in banana bunches and beach bar and beer-bloated me. The spinning nasties. A little cigarette smoke to clear the head, perhaps.

Returning Eth clashed crockery. Deliberately, I didn't wonder. Tea waterfalling into murky mugs. I sat up and blinked at the vertical world. Posture and the world aligned for one tenuous moment, then each tilted away from the other. I attempted the head in hands remedy – an appropriate admixture of penitence and hopelessness. Failure here also. My head tipping like a bucket awash with blood. Lie down again.

'Don't lie down!' Eth's concentration-camp voice. Most effective.

'I'm a sick man.' Pleading. Appeal to maternal sympathies.

'You're mentally sick. You and Charlie both. I've a good mind to call the police.'

'The police are men to a man. Except for the policewomen, who aren't.'

'I shall call them unless you drink this tea. Your last chance.'

'Please, kind sir,' – whining; everyone has a sense of humour – 'not the tea. I've a wife and kids. I'll go straight. I'll learn a trade. Plumbing, for example.'

'Stop buggering about.' Merciless. Eyes the same colour as the fingernails, only harder. Had a way of thinning her face from cheekbone downwards and compressing her lips to a hue-drained straightness without curve or compassion. Impossible to detect how it's done. The unsoft skull asserting itself through skin.

So I dipped my lips to the tea, flicking frequent glances at her to watch her fury cooking. Like a hostage monitoring the twitches of his psychopathic captor. Decided that the best way to soothe the situation was with an appearance of sobriety. A willingness to confront the issues. A demeanour befitting a senior Cabinet minister. I finally lit the debatable fag and shook the match out with a snake-shaped flourish of the wrist. I straightened my back and enquired loudly what her business was.

Eth was now sitting in my deckchair. Discomfiture in store for her but, at the moment, leaning back. Long legs crossed, right rocking lazily on pivotal left knee. Black-stockinged legs swimming all the way to an abbreviated skirt, like salmon going upstream. 'You,' she announced, 'are a sexist pig. In the eyes of the international sisterhood you are condemned.'

'Balls to the international sisterhood. The only things you've ever been interested in are getting a good job and getting laid. You'd steal your best friend's job and her boyfriend to boot.'

'I consider myself a feminist.'

'I could consider myself the natural heir to Lenin. It wouldn't make any difference.'

'Doing my job well is a political act.'

'Capitalism always has been.'

'And what the fuck are you doing about it? Sitting on

your arse drinking when you could be reading *Socialist Worker*? Selling corpses to the bourgeoisie?'

'I constitute the revolution's intellectual vanguard. Theoretical legitimation is logically prior to practice.' Slap down the sandbags of pomposity. See what comes hurtling over.

'If the revolution leaves from a pub, you'll be the last to join it.'

Bang. Then silence as the pieces subsided. A contemplative sip of tea as forces regroup on both sides. Eth quivering almost audibly, like the highest string of a violin strummed by a careless thumb. Diminishing zing. My head appearing gradually above the parapet.

'What sort of feminist have you become? Since Saturday night. I don't remember you being one then.'

'What sorts are there?'

Attempting to accumulate further evidence. Lure me into self-confession. Give it to her. 'Well, there's the professional wimmin. For whom men, ontologically, are irredeemable. There's the Greenham wimmin. For whom East-West relations are explicable in terms of the view that men have willies.' Pause for a vision of two ageing heavyweights flagellating each other to death with gigantic, flaccid members. 'Crèche activists, muesli terrorists, cycling saboteurs – *Guardian* readers, obviously. Liberal feminists, Tory feminists. The National Front probably has its fair share.'

'And?' Provocatively ignoring the provocation. Hands locked together at the knuckles and fingers forced down between palms. One hand temper, the other self-control. Or us. Unconscious metaphor transcending monosexualism. How very reassuring.

'And nothing. There must be sub-divisions within each sub-species. But you know them better than I do. Being a member of the internationale.'

'Male feminists. Some men get by without your shitty attitudes.'

28

'Please, no. Sidesplitting. Not me, sister.'

'You should try and think a little further than the last issue of *Private Eye*.'

'Min. Ranks of apologetic min. Contritely castrating themselves and handing their balls in at the nearest wimmin's centre.'

'This isn't funny.'

'Yes it is.'

'You've committed a crime against women. And all you can do is sit there pissing yourself.'

'A crime. If we're going to be melodramatic let's just call it a crime.'

Sudden silence in which we both breathed. Me feeling sleepy again, wishing she would go away. Not adequate to the unpredictable bounce of this dialogue. Wishing to be left immured in an unimportant existence, where my opinions and actions counted for nothing. The irresponsible life of an institutional prisoner, decisions made by necessity.

'You're a moral imbecile,' Eth declared. Objectively arrogant; a condemnatory summation. 'You sit about all day. You never go further than the pub. And when you do it's to perpetrate obscenities. I ought to go to the police.'

'I was an unwitting accomplice, damn you. It's Charlie you should be saying this to.' Desperate cry from the dock before being led downstairs. Trial as theatre, only the sentence being real. Hilarious montage of Eth in a judge's wig. Red curls bubbling under that punitive rectitude. Started laughing. Which only made things worse for myself.

'The only reason I'm not going to go to them is because they are men. As you so rightly say. The odd girl is neither here nor there where they're concerned.' Words ground out as though from a mincer, spewing slowly out on to a butcher's floor. Me watching the machinery of this determination. Scarlet-sawdust maggots of meat piling at my feet. Hilarity diminishing. 'But no one who dies like that

29

should die without leaving a trace. So I'm going to find out who she was. Then I'm going to find out who did it. And we'll take it from there.'

The plural pronoun exacted its toll. Standing at the entrance of something unknowable and demanding I pay – possibly a circus gypsy with hand outstretched for the mystery train. Companion, cuddle me; I never wanted this.

'I know why I'm doing it,' she said. 'You'd better invent the reasons why you're going to help me.'

5

If I could have run away from this I would. Escaped from this narrow, dog-shit neighbourhood, these houses piled aslant against the sky, the pale children sucking lollipops. From these cars which had shed every quality but their usefulness. And the drunks on the nearby green, their purple, greasy faces raving with reminiscence.

And from more than this. From embarrassing madmen cursing to their knees on late-night trains; from broken sofas in front gardens; from the unbearable shrieks of infants in supermarkets; from dry rubbish fixed in vegetable mud; from the tonnage of flesh flushed daily through the tubes, pressing its undisciplined, airless ranks together; from the sterile politeness of old women.

I would have escaped, even, from the blossoms of pornography which had suddenly burst forth – a couple of weeks ago – a mere street away. I remembered first seeing them – pages and pages of them – dispersed, displayed along the pavement so that it was possible to imagine that a medieval or pre-medieval massacre had taken place there, leaving behind those slaughtered segments of women's bodies. Strange flowers.

At the time they had struck me as nothing more than what they were – a bundle of magazines oddly discarded and scattered by the wind. But now they had a new significance – the significance of a clue or a premonition, almost. I seemed to recognise them as a general prophecy of the corpse I had unwillingly seen, clinging to lampposts, pressed up against walls. I wanted to escape from them too.

I dreamed of a journey as clear and as bare as a line on a map. To the south of France, there to live on bread and cheese and wine. Where the sun brushed the earth with the gracious punctuality of a slow electric fan. Where the grass was clean. A careless existence subsidised by small but nevertheless romantic crimes. Picking grapes when pockets didn't present themselves. The life of a philosopher vagabond, driven only by the breezes of my own impetuosity. Genet without the buggery. And free of this urban gravity.

But I had to make do with penury and lethargy. Two leaden entertainers. They taught me that it was possible to spread Marmite whilst semi-recumbent, as long as the loaf was pre-sliced. And to keep up with current events at the same time. A radio notified me of variations in the extramural world: variations in time or temperature, in statistics indicative of the nation's well-being, in the states of mind of various politicians. I discovered that I could stay in bed all day and all night as dullness and darkness swapped themselves around. Covering my face with old newspapers if the room became too bright. For a time my life seemed almost perfect. It possessed the unity and simplicity of a great work of art. One, perhaps, by Beckett.

Almost perfect. In every idyll the serpent plots, shrinking and sighing along its glittering scales until it has forethought its twisted drama. Mine was no different. I imagined Eth's tracks crossing and recrossing London. I saw her footprints superimposed on the city, as legible as a spoor in the snow. A winding search before she brought the story home to me. I saw her unappeasable fury uncoiling, receding then approaching in ceaseless spiralation. I knew that soon her steps would unwind to my door offering some fructified fact. Unearthed. A fact for me to bite on.

And then this peace – this existential hammock slung between my apathy and my daydreams – would be shaken and I would tumble all afluster to the earth. It was bound to happen soon; Eth wouldn't take for ever. And indeed she didn't, announcing herself with a ring at the doorbell that could only be hers: an extended, penetrative ring.

The doorbell's spike pierced me from ear to ear, and already I had started doing things. I stuffed my sullen arm into the olive-green dressing gown; and the other arm, strangely stiff at the shoulder. These joints of me, unused to such formality. And I ordered my legs to carry me to my visitor, at whom I stared with sadness. I remembered that for her, this call was in the nature of an unpleasant duty.

Eth circumvented me; I felt as absurd as the Maginot line. She pressed on down the hall to the staircase. And up the stairs, disappearing into the gloom like a ghost melting on the air, as though she had inhabited the place long before me and I was merely the solid intrusion. I pursued her into the kitchen where tomatoes and onions rolled beneath her hand on the breadboard. They were about to be potted, as in setting up a snooker table. Brown paper bags clumped together – the copse before the storm. I was going to be force fed. Must explain that I never eat on an empty stomach.

'When did you last have a proper meal?'

Searching the memory for her idea of a proper meal. Trying to visualise an executive dinner. Failing. 'Can't remember.'

'Shave?'

'Can't remember.'

'Wash?'

The response of the guilty congregation, chorusing, 'Can't remember.'

'You live like a fucking animal.' Incision through layers of lacrimatory onion. Dead skin ripped off. Sliced eyeball onion bleeding acidly. 'I'm going to make a spaghetti. I'm doing it for myself. But I'll let you have some.'

'Why this sudden surge of bullying? Are we going to the opera?'

'We're going on a tour of the local pubs. Much more to your taste, regrettably. Make yourself respectable.' Eth hurled a globe of mincemeat into an oiled pan. Where it slithered like a fat man on an ice rink.

'No hot water. No bath.'

'Shave then.'

I shuffled off to get dressed with the ingratitude of a patient being discharged from a disciplinarian hospital. By this harsh sister. I decided to look my best but found nothing ironed. My favourite shirt – grey silk like a shark's watered skin – had been crushed into the bottom of the lowest drawer – crumpled in on itself like a boxer doubled on a fist. I shook it out and sniffed at it. To a nasal inspection it seemed almost clean. One pair of denims also retrieved, folded for so long they had assumed parodic creases. Truly, I was regaining my self-respect. Like Dean Martin in *Rio Bravo*. And all it took was a good woman.

Through the connecting kitchen in bare feet to the bathroom. Expertly I agitated a bar of soap until it splurged lather on my hands. Transferred to jawbone and adjacent areas, where it formed a Santa's beard, deranged and sparse. The coldly damp razor slicing the stems of rooted, tugging hairs. My face as uncooperative as a hedgehog. This business of shaving was more a matter of force and persistence than delicacy. Scraped-over skin stinging pink and here and there a deeper, scarlet furrow. Quite wrong to treat one's faithful face that way.

This face. At which I looked, seeing it look back at me. The reflected face I could never see in repose, finding only

33

the face of me examining its face. Severed eternally from looking at myself in rest, discovering only a tensed or posing countenance prepared for scrutiny behind the glass. Eth saw me more accurately than the mirror did. I shouted to her:

'Do you find me handsome?'

The click and rustle of spaghetti stalks, bound in her fingers like a broom, stopped. Eth meditating. The answer was not obvious. 'No.'

'You had to think.'

'Handsome, yes. Attractive, no.'

'Explain.'

Stalks advanced to boiling water, there to become pliable. The purgatorial softening of the soul. Metaphor for. 'Too sculptural. You look as though you were put together by an art student. A Renaissance imitation.'

'Describe me.'

'Finely chiselled features.' Her little joke, prompting a snort of laughter. A horse tossing its head in the morning. 'His piercing blue eyes failed to transfix her beneath his mop of boyish yet greying hair. His long, aquiline nose – which she had once thought to be so attractive – proved to be an inconvenience during oral sex. A fine set of sparkling teeth tilted in his graveyard mouth like old tombstones. How does that sound?'

Patting the ploughed face dry, I removed the towel long enough to say, 'Deeply wounding.' Hooded myself again. Walked through the kitchen thus masked crying, 'Blind yet clean! Good citizen, have mercy!' Bumped into a wall and was led away. I went of my own volition in search of socks. And in due time returned, to discover Eth contemplating a squiggle of spaghetti adhering to the wall.

'If it sticks, it's ready,' she said.

Two empty plates, as greasy as fried eggs, on the table. Eth filled both our glasses with red wine. The solemn preparations for telling me what she knew. For explaining the next

34

step: which I was going to be compelled to take.

'I saw Nicola just before I paid my visit to you,' she began. 'That was how I found out about you and Charlie and your abhorrent arrangement.'

'Ah ha!' I interjected. 'You have given me much to work on.'

'Shut up. I've been back to see her since and she's told me more. She told me that she and Charlie had had a row the Thursday before the party. She was tired of his drugs, tired of his druggie friends, tired of having to support him. She was doing that fucking awful bar job to support him and he wasn't even interested in her. They hadn't screwed for weeks. All he did was lie on the floor and stick things up his nose.'

'That can be very sexual,' I suggested.

My psychotherapeutic intervention spurned. Eth's exegesis extending. 'So she went out. She said she didn't have anywhere particular in mind. She wanted to find somewhere quiet, have a few drinks, think things over.'

'Dangerous,' I said. 'Thinking and drinking. Especially when frustrated.'

'She had one drink too many and she decided to come down here to see you. That's how desperate she was.'

'Bad form to fuck one's best friend's lady. I would have firmly refused to satiate her inebriated lusts.' A supercilious maxim from Angelo's book of etiquette.

'And she got here and you didn't answer. You were either playing dead or out drinking. Which ever it was, you wouldn't have been any use to her.' Eth poured herself another glass of wine. Her hand was unnecessarily steady. As though she were balancing a form of words also in her hand. Like a duellist slowly weighing a sword. 'I think it was then,' she continued, 'that she realised that the problem was not you or Charlie or any one man specifically. It was all men in general. She had finally appreciated that men are never there when you want them.'

'The road to Damascus leads past my door. How very portentous.'

'Something had changed. Something you can't even begin to understand.' Eth peering at me dramatically. My consciousness was about to be raised. Or merely expanded. 'She drifted round the pubs in this part of the world. But she wasn't worrying about Charlie any more and she wasn't looking for you. She was looking for a woman.'

Silence. This Nicola not the one I knew. Reversed by a flip of the fingers, like a card in a magician's hand. I couldn't bring myself to believe in it. Although having seen this switch. Or heard it spoken of. 'That simple,' I muttered. 'And that simply.'

'You should see the look on your face,' Eth chortled victoriously. A coup for her, assuredly. 'You look as though you've just realised you've had your pockets picked.'

Astute lady, I mentally conceded. A drum roll on the table with my fingertips; to mark the end of this interlude. I assumed once more a Holmesian detachment: 'Your story, madam, contains several points of singular interest. From the fact that you have not finished I deduce that there is more to tell. Please continue, omitting nothing, however trivial it may seem to you.'

Eth's story riding out this stream of Victorian fatuity. Paddled her own canoe. 'It got to eleven o'clock and she was at the desolate drunk stage. When you start crying as long as there's somebody to cry to. But she couldn't do it by herself so she wandered along to the Nile.'

'Which,' I commented, 'is full of alligators.'

'She didn't care. She told me she was so miserable she really didn't give a damn. She couldn't have cared less what happened to her. She was sitting at the bar when she met Karen.'

'The girl?' Named at last.

Eth nodded. Emerald eyes dulled to the colour of a rain-washed privet hedge, as though stupefied by the narrative grinding out between us but unable to halt the horrific idiocy of what she was repeating. Like watching someone being pulled into a threshing machine. 'She never discovered her last name. Karen talked about men, how much she hated them. It suited Nicola's state of mind, so she listened. That's all.' A dismissive gesture, as if she was resigned to coaxing the figure no further from the shadows.

'What did she look like?' I asked. Remembering the body only as a chalk line round a body. An indication surrounding a blankness, where something had been.

'Nicola gave me what I would call a police description: five foot six; straight blonde shoulder-length hair; blue eyes; slim build; late teens. That sort of thing.'

'The most unhelpful kind of description there is. Rather like describing a meal by saying it was served on plates.' Straight to the skin of the matter. Anatomise further. 'Did they spend all their time inveighing against men? No light chit-chat. About cricket, for example?'

'She gave the impression that she'd come to London very recently. Perhaps from up North. But Nicola can't identify accents – she's never been further than Birmingham.' Tapped an empty wine glass against her lower teeth. The arhythmic tinging of a faulty telephone. 'And she usually worked evenings. But this was an evening off.'

Me still trying to make out the shape scuttling in the shadows. 'What as?'

She rolled the stem of her wine glass, half-descended to the table, between index finger and thumb. Looking at me as though she wanted to be sure of her timing. A surfer gauging the waves, holding back for a sufficient tide of sympathy. Or a doorstep conman, assessing the gullibility of a housewife. The latter closer to it.

Realisation. I was about to have an ordinary shabbiness foisted on me as tragic grandeur. Granted myself permission to smile a sour, downturned smile. 'Poor girl,' I said. 'Poor Nicola. And, lastly, poor you. When did she find out?'

'Not until Saturday evening. Karen explained that she was very tired that night, so Nicola invited her to the party. She thought it would be an appropriate public humiliation

37

for Charlie. They arranged to meet in a West End pub. The girl turned up and stated her fees.'

I imagined Nicola sitting with hands folded over her handbag. Clicking the clasp, grasping the misunderstanding – hoping no one had overheard this contractual discourse. And wanting not to provoke the form of disturbance known as a scene.

'She refused to pay her a penny, of course.'

'Such a delicate morality. Highly commendable.'

'But Karen started talking about what would happen to her if she went back without any money and Nicola realised it was her duty to provide some sort of protection. The solidarity of sisterhood.'

'And we know how it ended.'

'Sold by men; murdered by men; and sold by men again. Don't forget your part in all this.'

'That's your sexual paranoia. I'm as innocent as a new-born babe.'

'You were born a man.'

'Ostensibly.'

'And now' – Eth standing up; rising with a sweep intended to incorporate me in its impetus – 'we're going on our tour of the local pubs. We're going to find out more about the girl.'

'How?' Paper-clip question snapped at the back of a teacher's neck. Pinging her naïvety.

'Ask around.'

Laughter hacking out of my throat, sounding like an axe rebounding off a hollow tree. 'Ask around!' Puffing out the words as though disowning a heresy. 'That jungle of thugs, pimps and prostitutes and you're going to ask around!'

Eth as unperturbed as a Protestant. 'No,' she said. 'We are.'

6

Down the streets of the uncontrollable city. I had a vertiginous vision – me flying high above the city and it spread out beneath me like a giant's body. Afflicted with unceasing, tiny twitches and convulsive muscles slapping on the earth. Treated by ECT for the ills of its mind. I turned and said to Eth –

'Do you know why you think you can find things out?'

'Yes.' Curt answer. She was still annoyed with me.

'It's because you believe there are reasons for things. As in this case. You think there was a motive.'

'People don't go around killing each other for no reason.'

'Yes they do. Peter Sutcliffe, Dennis Nielson . . . In the States practically everyone does it.'

We stopped on the pavement, at a point bisecting two street lights. Ideal for muggings and the like. 'You're not getting out of this. Either we do it or the police do it. Your choice.'

'You don't understand. What if it was done entirely at random?' My palms flat, slicing the air sideways. Cutting a flat slate through the night. 'Utterly without cause, sense or justice? A psychopath's weekend entertainment? Let me tell you something – '

'We are going to find out.' A simple statement of intent. Words like a claw poised to land. A talon tense in the sky. And Eth's face hooked towards me in the dark, as though her determination alone were sufficient to surmount the otherwise insuperable obstacles of silence and confusion in this dumb or jumbled organism. Where we were.

Took five small paces. Thinking. How to minimise the damage, which I viewed as inevitable. Concluded. 'We'll go to the Nile later. When it's full. The pimps drink in the Pacific and the Regent. They're the obvious ones to start with. But first we can go for a pint in the local. If we're going drinking I'll need a drink first.'

And we duly did. I informed Eth as to strategy, drawn up primarily for self-protection and with the eliciting of information only as a secondary aim. Namely: that Karen was a friend of hers, last heard of in this vicinity; that one always surveyed exits, bearing in mind that access to one should remain unimpeded; that one did not venture into lavatories, as this could put one at a disadvantage when accosted; that, on being assaulted, one made a lot of noise prior to running like hell. And, this not being a Clint Eastwood movie, the principle of devil take the arsemost was fully operative.

To the Pacific. Tiled outside with maroon tiles. A good wall for pissing and banging heads against. Inside not much different. To the right of the door, the Irish. Building workers with mortar-dusted arms and faces that looked as if they had been roughly fashioned from left-over cement. The women at a separate table, huddled in communal confession of their husbands' sins. To the left, the blacks. Heavy-faced Rastas, ganjaed in exile, their voices rolling beneath the level of my hearing. And girls with braided, beaded hair, boredly eating crisps.

Eth and I promenading up the middle. She looking too damned expensive, I knew it. To the bar, where the professionals sat. Lightweight suits hung on them like flags of convenience. Reptilian shoes, tucked on the stools' struts, pointed snout-downwards. Two fedoras tilted forward, casting shadows to the nose-tip like visors, behind which eyes surveyed us. And sheen-shined handkerchiefs spouting over breast pockets. I considered this to be a cliché – pimps and shysters setting out to be pimps and shysters. In the manner of dress prominently. Tradition or television – who could tell?

I insisted on ordering and paying myself. To command respect; essential in such circumstances and circles. Be seen to live off a woman's earnings and these bastards would show no deference. Which they never did anyway. Hoped

40

Eth understood that expediency alone dictated this.

She patronised the bar at an acute angle. 'Excuse me,' she said to the barmaid's back. An unresponsive back, hunched slightly at the shoulders, covered in a pale blue T-shirt, attending to a roundabout of inverted spirit bottles.

One of the professionals tapped on the teak counter with the edge of a coin. A sound like a blind man's stick in an alley, I reflected. Thinking of Blind Pew, the distributor of destiny. The back turned round, showing a front that was effectively concave. A broad, flat face with dead hair falling straight on either side. Partially bleached and resembling burnt straw. 'Carol,' the professional said, blunt finger gliding Ethwards from his fist, 'the lady wants to speak to you.'

The barmaid didn't speak. She stood, hands on hips, facing Eth. Long length of lips, painted pale, stretched perfectly horizontal. Eyes like cold cod on a fishmonger's slab. Eth smiled her salaried smile – the one that worked every day for her in that bizarre – what? – institution? – where her manifold roles seemed to include that of public relations. But it didn't work here. Length of opposing lip untroubled by even a tremble. 'I'm looking for a friend,' said Eth. 'I wonder if you know where she lives.'

More silence. To which too many people were listening.

Eth proceeded to describe her. The police description, whose style – if not the person to whom it referred – was bound to be recognised. At least, I fervently hoped that would prove to be the case. Then the description ended and the barmaid was still standing with her slaughtered eyes.

'Say something, Carol,' said one of the professionals. 'Ask the lady what the girl's name is.'

'What's the girl's name?' asked Carol. Her voice creaked like a door being pushed slowly shut.

I saw the first mistake coming. A hearse on the crest of a hill. With no brakes. Innocent Eth at the wheel and the contraption now well and truly trundling as she said, 'Karen.'

41

It's impossible to be sure now, but I believe Carol actually grinned. If so, it was a brief, upward distortion of the mouth – as though the corners had been twitched by strings.

'Ask her another question,' prompted a voice from underneath a hat brim. 'Ask her what the girl does.'

'What does she do?' Carol intoned obediently.

Eth's poise suddenly vanished behind a cloud of embarrassed fluster; a pinkish, evening cloud, as of someone who's been caught shoplifting. I could see the wrong words rushing to her lips, could hear them uttered even, and to my ears they sounded like the smash and crumple of a last collision. She said –

'She tricks Johns.'

Carol returned to rotate her roundabout and the professionals' laughter rippled like rubber tyres on tarmac. There was much slow digging of elbows into ribs. The only question that remained was how to negotiate an exit that was both hasty and dignified. I took a temporising sip and considered. Eth was perplexed as to the nature of her indiscretion. The laughter had stopped and a sense of imminence pervaded the suspended conversation, as when, at a dinner party, a guest has wilfully exposed himself and one waits for a verbal salvation. I remembered that the *Reader's Digest* commended the Messianic properties of humour.

'Good people!' I began. 'My acquaintance is distressed by a recent bereavement and has lost her memory for names. I regret that, when she recalls them at all, they are invariably wrong. The girl whom she seeks is in fact called Desmond and the pub she frequents is the Wide Sargasso Sea. I thank you for your time and attention. I shall not insult you by purchasing a round.' A deep bow and a courtly smile. God helps those who can't help themselves. Trust they are aware of this proverb, lest His wrath fall on their fedoras.

I seized Eth by the elbow and towed her to the door. An ungainly waltz. Observed the glances we received and was pleased to see that they were full of pity: the pity reserved for lunatic white trash and the aristocracy. Out on to the no less dangerous street, and left turn for home.

Eth stopped. She anchored herself to the pavement with a barnacular fixity. 'What the fuck are you playing at?' An onset of Italianate gesturing. I judged that she was annoyed, knowing that she had mismanaged the situation but not quite knowing how. 'What the fuck was that about?'

'You don't,' I told her, 'trick Johns. You turn tricks. And the first one – that was a trick question too. Complicated, isn't it?' Like explaining to her the way kerbside card sharps worked. Fleeced at find the lady. 'I realised as soon as he told the barmaid to ask it. The girl would only have given Nicola her professional name. Not the real one. Just the one she operated under.'

'So?'

'So she couldn't have been your friend. Otherwise you would have used the other one. Whatever it was.' I reasserted my grip of her. She came unstuck from the pavement.

'Shit.'

'Exactly.' Pause. 'What we're in.' Pause. 'We're being followed.'

I had always had an instinct for when I was being followed. Derived, I supposed, from acting. That exact sense of personal placement, coupled with an ability to distinguish between two nigh identical phenomena: the accidental, incidental stroll of a meaningless pedestrian and the pursuer's deliberate, tentative tread.

'What do we do?' Eth was more concerned than frightened. She wanted to get it right this time – assuming that there was some correct procedure of which I might be aware; some magical, trapdoor exit from this hazardous stage.

'Nothing,' I said. 'If we run, they'll run faster. If we turn into a back street we'll make it easier for them. If we hide in

43

a doorway, easier still. Keep calm. Be polite. Be helpful. Resistance is useless. We can but preserve the social proprieties. Like dressing for dinner in the jungle.' Advocating the gracious acceptance of defeat. A speciality of mine.

Four figures mingled with ours. As easeful, unstoppable and forceful as the bonding of atoms in a chemical chain. A hand on my shoulder, its extended fingers crooking and driving under the clavicle. 'Man,' – a voice whispering warmly past my ear, dissipating along the unlit road – 'you're coming with us.'

'My companion?' I enquired. 'What of her?' A touch of malice here, but I was reluctant to let the catalyst of this fizzy little conjunction get away.

'Yeah.' As though it hadn't occurred to him. Sprung in his mind at my suggestion. 'Why not? Her too.'

Headlights stared bigger from the opposite direction. Silver-white lights starring in my eyes. The vehicle of my premonitions was approaching. And Eth was standing still again, swathed in its saintly beams. She seemed equipped for this eventuality only with the simplicity of a martyr. Her face had the marmoreal clarity of a Bernini statue as she endured this revelation.

The car halted and its rear door swung phantasmically open. A red Mercedes coupé inviting us to its leather.

'Get in.'

The hand unwrapped from my clavicle and splayed between my shoulder-blades. Eth was also being shoved. We scrambled in like kids on the way to a picnic. The door shut and locked automatically. To stop the kids tumbling out.

Recounting to myself the various tortures which the criminal classes were reputed to inflict on their poorly esteemed members, I gazed out of the car window at the free world. This, I assured myself, was no worse than going to the dentist. More painful – that was the only difference. I needed something to soothe the nerves. I addressed our silent chauffeur. 'Mind if I smoke?'

'You burst into flames if you want.' He cackled delightedly at his own wit. 'You want a drink?'

'Sure,' I said. Could almost get to like being kidnapped.

The driver steered with one hand as he tugged a half-bottle out of his hip pocket. He passed it back to me without looking round. Scotch. I wondered how much I could take whilst remaining within the bounds of good manners, and judged that, in this new atmosphere of conviviality, a substantial shot was in order. And to enquire whither we were tending.

'You go around asking questions,' he informed me, 'and people ask you questions. I ring up Willy right away and tell him and Willy says he wants to speak to you. So now we going to the Nile so he can speak to you all he wants. I drive you there because he tells me to.' Arm stretching over, fingers clicking. Bottle returned. 'I don't want to drive you around. Your chick's a fucking nuisance, man.'

He parked savagely outside the Nile, running the car up the pavement as if he were beaching a boat, and shooed us through the door like chickens into an interior that could be described as unpretentious. The sort of plastic chairs that belong in comprehensive schools. And plastic beakers, which cause little injury if hurled. A woman slashed with scarlet make-up stared at us, unsure whether we were privileged guests or hostages; resentful anyhow as we were ushered into Willy's prohibited office.

A beige sofa curved in the near left corner like a caterpillar. In the right, four fractured card tables were stacked. There was an olive green filing cabinet further along the wall, its top drawer open and full of wire coathangers. No windows. And a pair of armchairs, like frogs waiting for a fly, crouched in the middle of the bare floor. They were expecting us. We sat down.

Willy contemplated us both for a long time and, during that surgical pause, I recollected what I'd heard about him. He was a man whose reputation didn't so much precede him as swirl around him. I had caught his name, twice or thrice, whispered amidst the cigarette smoke of a pub conversation; I'd listened to an exchange on the tube where, between the rush and the rattles, it was audible again. And, on one occasion, late at night, I had heard the phrase, 'Willy says so! Willy says so!' shouted urgently down the street. And there were rumours: he owned a used car lot in Peckham; he ran a highly profitable string of whores (or was it horses?); he had patented a new method for the disposal of scrap-metal; he sometimes committed acts of extravagant charity. And once, just once, I had seen him in a bookshop – his great brow creased over a thick volume open in his palms. I had judiciously manoeuvred myself so as to be able to read its title (expecting it to be, say, the latest Trevor Mudlumb); but it had turned out to be a Greek-English lexicon. His index finger was running through the alphas.

Now, however, he was wearing heavily tinted glasses and looked as if he had two steel shutters drawn down from his eyebrows. His bald head reflected the trio of spotlights above and behind it, so that it resembled a glazed pot. A short, dense beard – the sort of beard that could be used for scrubbing pans – grew wirily along his jawbone. His desk was empty except for one internal and one external telephone, and a framed photograph slanted towards him. It was the desk of a man who conducted his affairs with a tidiness merging into invisibility. At length, he heaved himself forward in his swivel chair and spoke –

'You probably think I am a very bad man. But then, you are a very bad detective. You have endangered yourself and this woman.' Hand spreading out slowly, like a sea anemone unfurling, to indicate Eth, who was sulking inside her coat. 'Your youthful efforts have uncovered nothing. Only I have benefited from them.' A dignified, arrogant articulation, pronounced with the meditative certainty of a village elder. Each word was carefully shaped, as though he were blowing glass bubbles. 'Do you think it is right of me to say this?'

'It's your show, brother,' I told him. 'You say what you want.'

'Please, do not call me brother.' A slight acceleration there. But outwardly he remained unmoved, his flamingo pink shirt unruffled, its stiff billows puffed out along his arms from beneath his grey waistcoat. 'Do you think I am a bad man?' he asked.

'Not at all,' I replied. 'Far from it.'

'Ah. So many people do. Amongst both my own and your people.' He drew the photograph on the desk closer to him. Then he stood up and brought it over to me with the thoughtful air of a barrister approaching a witness, his substantial stomach undulating before him. 'My family, Mr Paris. I am a family man.' As who wasn't, in his line of work?

It had been posed by a portrait professional. A quintet of faces, tickled into smiles by some glib trick; mother and father eagerly proud at the rear, two girls and a boy uncomfortably prettied to the fore. The composition vaguely reminded me of jellied fruit. I grunted at it with a sound ambiguous enough to be construed as admiration.

Willy withdrew the photograph and balanced himself on the edge of the desk, almost spilling off, like too much blancmange quivering on a spoon. 'My son, Samuel,' he went on, 'is lazy at school. He is sure he will inherit the benefits of his father's labour, therefore he wastes his own

47

and his teachers' time. Consequently, I am compelled to
supervise his studies. This week we are reading together a
play by your poet Shakespeare, called *The Merchant of
Venice*. It has impressed me as a most enlightened work. It
deals with something which concerns me closely: the ways
in which men make money.' A bitter-sweet smile at this
mild self-denigration. 'The predicament of the Jew,' he
continued, 'is similar to my own in many respects. He must
survive in a society which is inimical to him. He must do
things which are deemed distasteful and, because of this,
he is despised. You see that there is some inconsistency of
attitude here?'

There was much to be said, but none of it was worth
saying then. I hoped that silence would afflict Eth also: an
infection more acceptable than a rash outbreak of wimmin-
ism, under these circumstances. I nodded.

Willy paused, presumably to judge the sincerity of my
assent, before continuing, 'My son, Samuel, has been set a
question to answer: "Is *The Merchant of Venice* a tragedy?"
What do you think he should write, Mr Paris?'

I tried to frame a reply which would neither feed his
vanity nor insult him. 'Shylock,' I said, 'was just a money-
lender. Not a prince. Not a general.'

'The same contempt' – blunt finger prodding downwards through the air – 'the same contempt. You consider
me to be a shark. A flesh-eating animal. But then, my
ancestors were cannibals, were they not, Mr Paris? Niggers
with bones through their noses and a priest in the pot?' The
words flicked me like sawdust and splinters flying off his
tongue. His own anger had enraged him. 'I trust I don't
offend you by using the word nigger?'

Eth, beside me, was about to speak – a sudden rigidity
shooting up her spine, as though a syringe had stabbed her
nervous system. She stated the obvious – of which I had
lost sight – in an unmodulated, middle-pitched note; like a
flute blown once and hard. 'You sell women on street
corners.'

Willy's face stayed turned to mine. Not, I speculated, a deliberate provocation, more the old habit of assuming that this was men's business. 'Your young lady,' he said, 'is very naïve. She sees only one side of the story. I doubt if she has stood on Euston station on a Saturday morning and watched these girls leaving the train. They have come from Liverpool, or Manchester maybe. I do not know. They have no money, they have no friends, they have nowhere to stay. They imagine they will become waitresses and meet singing stars or actors. The reality, of course, is different. They are merely driven from one despair to another.'

And then, addressing Eth for the first time: 'Shall I tell you what we call these girls? We call them Thatcher's girls. Your Mrs Thatcher – whom I believe to be a woman – is our biggest provider of prostitutes. And I shall tell you something else, young lady; something I have often noted to be the case. Your people do not object as long as a black man deals in black girls. You think it is expedient to preach solely when you see a black man dealing in white pussy.'

'I can't stand this. You make me feel ill.' She looked as though this were no rhetorical trope either. 'I'm leaving.'

'The door is not locked,' said Willy. 'I brought you here because you expressed concern about someone whom you called Karen. I, too, am worried as to where she may be. It is possible we can help each other. But no one will stop you if you wish to leave. If your concern for this Karen is so small.'

He returned to his swivel chair. The wall behind him was papered dark blue, with great orange circles patterned on it like a child's crayoning of the sky repeated and repeated. Signed photographs of half a dozen obscure boxers were ranged at head height. I recognised none of their faces – those comic masks fixed for the camera, the grins tacked up across bruise-bloated mugs.

'I care for my girls,' said Willy. 'If one goes missing, I want to find her. This one,' he added, 'especially.'

'Flesh is money. Pound for pound.' Ironic Eth spitting aphorisms.

'If you genuinely desire to find her, Miss Spurgeon, I shall assist you. If your desire is not genuine, I request you to go.'

I'm sure that, had Eth been wearing gloves, she would at this point have adjusted them delicately on her fingers. She reacted, in all other respects, like some great lady confronted by a blackmailer. Her nose up-tilted exquisitely, as though avoiding an odour from the kitchens, and she enquired with quiet distaste, 'What do you want?'

'I want you simply to refer your discoveries to me. In exchange I shall give you the girl's address and a sum of money. Researches of this kind can be expensive, entailing much contact with avaricious people. Is this arrangement fair?'

'Her name.' He'd made it clear enough he knew our names. 'We need her real name.'

'It is a matter of professional tact that we do not deal in our girls' real names. We never ask because no one would ever tell us. These girls like to think of their occupation as a charade in which they themselves are not truly participating. The concealment of names aids this pretence. Her address, though, I shall give you.'

'And the money.' In a swift and puzzling reversal Eth had become the avaricious one.

'The money too. One hundred pounds, and more when you require it.'

'For which you want her returned. Bound and gagged.'

'No,' said Willy. 'Your task is only to find her. I trust you for nothing greater.' He examined his thumbnail as though it were a semi-precious stone, turning it under the lamplight until it reflected almost opalescent; then, when he was satisfied, he tossed me a prepared envelope.

I unsealed it. It contained a neat square of paper, and a house number and local street were inscribed on it in deliberate capital lettering. And one hundred pounds – the same sum as Charlie had received. Wanted dead or alive – reward identical. So the interview was over, except for one detail.

'You said I was a bad detective. Can't you find anyone better?'

Willy smiled with genuine amusement. 'I can find no one more innocent,' he told me. 'No one who looks less like a criminal and, consequently, no one who looks less like a policeman. But, above all, I can find nobody whiter. You can go where my people can't.'

Walking back, I waved the envelope at Eth. 'Dirty money,' I said. 'As dirty as you can get. None dirtier,' I added, for emphasis.

'He doesn't know she's dead.'

'And that keeps you in the clear, does it?'

'It means we tricked him. We got something for nothing.'

'We haven't tricked him for ever. He'll have to be told sooner or later.'

We stopped at a late-night supermarket. Slices of fluorescent light fell on the pavement outside, and inside the till girls were blanched like corpses. This shop like a vast fridge, preserving people and food in its icy box. We passed between tins stepped on shelves and freezers stuffed with bags and cartons. The material with which I sustained myself massed here; the material of which I was made – packaged, pickled and cold. A mortuary of food. I turned, turned, turned again; down the aisles towards the Scotch.

'I'd forgotten how wonderful it was,' I told Eth. 'Out of the strong came forth sweetness.'

'Who's paying for this?'

'From communal funds. I invite you to my abode to partake of the pleasures.'

I paid the assistant. She laid the bottle down and twisted it in white tissue, so that it looked like a mummy in its ribbon. A stiff drink, I thought, ha, ha. I tucked the embalmed fluid under my arm and departed for home, Eth's tapered heels clicking behind me like an alarm clock in an insomniac's night.

And eventually I was sitting in my deckchair, a filled

glass beside me on the floor and a plurality of cigarettes in my pocket. It should have been a time of contentment; the basic requirements of my diminished existence were all present. But I wasn't happy. I felt like butter spread too thinly, or a ball of cotton wool spun into separate strands. It was because these connections, these proliferating contacts, made me feel fragmented – as though I had shared out my identity between strangers, scattered it in pubs and clubs. I wished I could gather myself into a plastic bag and take it somewhere quiet. My only possession.

And Eth was standing behind me. I could tell she was thinking. I could sense her hovering above her mind like a kingfisher poised by a pond, waiting for a fish to touch the surface.

'Sex,' she announced, 'is out of the question.'

It was one of Eth's less endearing habits – telling me that she wasn't available when I had no intention of availing myself. 'Absolutely,' I said. 'Feminists don't do that sort of thing.'

'You're being stupid. Sex is a complicated transaction. You can't just decide that you're going to be a lesbian even if you want to. Women are made to depend on men, so you end up desiring something you hate. Like every type of addiction.'

'Sex,' I repeated, 'is a complicated transaction. Nicola was prepared to have it for free, but she wouldn't pay for it. It's the only form of exchange I'm aware of where the acceptance of charity is regarded as positively respectable.'

'There are other ways of paying than money.' A weary, midnight voice.

'Oh, we have all suffered so much.' In lugubrious tones, as of a great Chekhovian lady reviewing her life. 'We have all endured so much. And for so long.'

'You know damn well what I mean. Apart from the statistics for sexual diseases, unwanted pregnancies, broken marriages, wife-beatings, child abuse, suicides and marital murders – apart from that you still know what I mean.'

'You must have thought it was worth it.'

Six summers ago. When I had been with a company touring university theatres on minimum Equity rates, awakening the proletariat to a consciousness of its historical role by way of a drama entitled *Samantha's Self-Discovery*. In which a black girl left her husband and unionised the apathetic workers of a button factory, overcoming between those termini every form of prejudice which capitalism and the playwright had conspired to invent. It was a sort of Trotskyite *Pilgrim's Progress*, in which the scissors of socialism snipped her burdens one by one from her back. I played an Apollyonic patriarch who waylaid her phallically in the shop floor valley of machinery. It was my function to be slain by a single sentence as, by this time, Sam and her sisters had discovered nearly all of themselves.

We failed to awaken the proletariat – due mainly, we believed, to the fact that the capitalist media had refused to notice our searing indictment of etc., etc. – but managed to hold instead a series of charming post-performance discussion groups. The author – Sue Spender – would begin by apologising to women throughout the world for the fact that there were men in the cast, and would then go on to exculpate herself on the grounds that only men could possibly impersonate their own evil. Myself and other males, hands folded in our laps, would induce expressions of shame and guilt, like broken defendants at a show trial. The prosecutrix general would proceed to give her reasons for not making it clear that Sam had become a vegetarian by the end of the last act. ('Might alienate black, working-class women, some of whom are denied free access to vegetables.') Or why she hadn't dealt with the position of gays in trade unions. ('Enough plays on that subject already. For example, *The Importance of Being Albert*.')

Then, one fateful night, as we sat around the stage in our

53

favourite non-sexist formation, I was asked, 'How do you feel about this play – as a man?'

I thought carefully. Here was my chance to cleanse my soul in full confession. I looked at those student faces, theories bursting out of them like pimples. Those sincere Spotskyites, yearning to side with Sue. Those Acnarchists, avid for purgation – urgent that I should name min's sins so that we could join together in acts of contrition and groans of self-abasement. 'Women – ' I declared, 'they each have a little mind of their own. They each have their own little personality. Sometimes you can almost believe they understand every word you say. But, as playwrights, they're fucking awful.'

Wicked Angelo stalked out with mephistophelean strides. I had deduced from the squawks behind me that I had already become a devil. I crossed the campus to the bar, where I spied a girl sitting singly with an orange juice; amidst this comingling of baggy-jumpered chemists and baggy-minded sociologists, no bad decision either. Brandishing my beer like a toasting fork, I joined her.

'I've just lost my faith,' she slurred. That orange juice wasn't uncontaminated.

'What in?' I enquired solicitously.

'The Church of England.'

'In that case,' I suggested, 'it wasn't much to lose.'

'Ah, ha!' she cried, shaking a slim finger at me like a victorious logician. 'What am I going to believe in next?'

'Haven't a clue,' I said. 'Why don't you try Satanism?'

'Do you know what it's like?' she demanded. 'Being without faith?'

'Rather like,' I proposed neatly, 'being an actor without a part. Which happens to be my position.'

So, by the coincidence of simultaneous loss, we collapsed into each other's lives. And replayed that collapse; as when, on a film clip, a chimney stack is exploded, resurrected and exploded. We emerged and re-emerged in each other's lives with a certain irrepressibleness, like two swimmers inanely and repetitiously ducking one another. On a station platform, at a party, in a shop, I never felt completely safe from Eth.

Mutatory Eth, an inveterate supporter of causes. I remembered that, three years ago, her enthusiasm for CND had mushroomed at the same time as its national membership had grown; now they had fallen out. And before that she had been in the Conservative Party, for whom her mother was a prominent flower arranger. And prior to that her most vocal allegiance was to the International Babyfood Action Network, a group dedicated to the worldwide subversion of Coca-Cola Ltd. She was consistent only in that she had always been the noisy advocate of one protestation or another. And, consequently, I had become adept at consigning all her faiths to the dustbin assumption that she had to believe in something. It was the existential datum appropriate to her – that without which she couldn't survive, as cream buns or adulation were for other people.

And sex. There had been occurrences of sex. The occasional, disoriented firefight between guerrillas blind at night. The first time on the carpet of her university apartment – a room in a tower block named after Sir Walter Ralegh. I reckoned we were about in Sir Walter Ralegh's armpit. And she had flopped up and down on top of me like an expiring fish, shouting 'When I want to do it' – groin grinding down – 'you're fucking drunk' – never knew human beings had so many edges – 'what fucking use is that?' – she must be getting something out of this – 'you're going limp inside me now, you bastard' – violent crack as pelvic bones collide – 'I don't know why I fucking bother.' I lit a cigarette and contemplated the contortions rage ploughed across her face.

And the second time. In the changing rooms of a department store, a curtain to the ankles concealing us from the commercial world. My height proved to be an encumbrance, but at least we were both standing up. Her shoulder-blades banging against the mirror and the mirror

showing me the expressions of a Sicilian bandit consu-
mating a vendetta. A savage's lust to prove that a debt
could be paid. As it finally was, when the cubicle
shuddered, and it smelt as though a tin of anchovies had
been poured down both our legs. Eth later returned a pair
of jeans to the manageress, a middle-aged lady with a
uniform and demeanour akin to those of a ward sister.

Or on the linoleum floor of a professor's bathroom,
having absconded from a dissertation on Aristotle's *Poetics*.
Adopting, in deference to the circumstances, a trochaic
metre for our activities. And we had returned, light-legged,
to discover a debate on cannibalism in the classical world
taking place amidst the canapés.

And other occasions, ludicrous and spasmodic, when I
had been ambushed by appetite. Never in an aeroplane
though. And never, to the best of my recollection, in bed.

As the memories jolted past, like houses seen from a
train, Eth had been standing silently, staring at the
curtains. Her mind like a road beside a railway track;
parallel, divergent, curving back to cross over a bridge and
divergent again. She said –

'I never thought any of it was worth it. You used to use
me and leave me like a public lavatory. Dropping in with
your flies undone and doing them up on the way out.
Whenever you were in need or even when you were just
bored. I may write a book about us one day. I'll call it
Bruising Encounters in Unlikely Places.'

'Men make history; women rewrite it.' As though it were
a fact which neither of us could avoid.

'I'm finding out,' she said. 'I'm trying to find out what
history you did make. You and Charlie and the man who
bought the body. And whoever killed her. What you
conspired to invent.'

'And tomorrow?'

'Tomorrow you're going to go to that address.'

'And tonight?'

'Tonight you're sleeping on the floor. It's too late for me
to go home.'

8

A night like an incomplete mosaic. Dreams like tiny tessera dappled across sleep's black wall, this fragment or that flaking away to flutter through consciousness. Shards of nightmare in their smoky colours, as though seen from behind a guttering oil lamp, and me like an archaeologist in this dome of undiscovered dreams. Five times, or maybe four, I woke with an arid shakiness, reached for the whisky and slurped in the darkness.

Day substituted itself subtly, sliding into the gaps night left as it receded. At about seven-thirty I decided that it was impossible to prolong my punctuated sleep further and creaked myself upwards from the floorboards. I found that Eth had appropriated my dressing gown and was already occupying the kitchen. Her milky, unmade-up face looked as though it was dripping into her bowl of cornflakes. She greeted me between munches. I decided to try to hold a normal conversation.

'What are you doing today?'

'Entertaining the Anti-Terrorist Squad.'

I should point out that Eth worked for a charitable organisation which had been founded in the 1930s by a gentle Fabian. She had omitted to die but, as a kind of compensation, had been ennobled. Now, as Lady Thruckston, she sat twittering on the benches of the Lords, occasionally rising to reminisce about people and causes long forgotten. Her monument, however, was the Home for Miners' Widows which – in her at least mental absence –

had first been hijacked from its rural location to Battersea and then renamed the Centre for Victims of Male Violence. So, where once it had been staffed by nurses for the care of elderly and baffled ladies, it was now run by women for women; and Eth and her colleagues seemed to view it as a guerrilla training camp – a place where casualties could be re-equipped.

'The Anti-Terrorist Squad?'

'They're doing a sponsored bike ride for us. I've got to write a short press release, then keep them happy over lunch. Which means keeping them oiled.'

'Like their bikes.'

'The cogs of justice whizzing round.'

'And the big wheels in motion.'

'Why are they doing it for you?' I asked, with the self-conscious tone of someone trying to be idiomatically affable. Like a doctor chatting to a patient whilst cutting off a cast.

'They like to do these publicity stunts. It gets them in the news and everyone thinks what splendid chaps they are. Heroes with hearts of gold. That sort of crap. Besides – ' Eth's eyes levelled at mine.

'Besides?' My newly practised amiability was being challenged.

'After last month's report on sexism in the police, it looks good if they do a benefit for a women's refuge.'

'You get the cheque. They surface with an odour as of roses. Joyfulness abounds.'

'That's how it works. Policemen pedalling in circles for the good of all.'

'And why the Anti-Terrorist Squad?'

'Because,' said Eth, 'they don't have anything else to do.'

She glanced at her wrist – on which there was no watch, automatically announced, 'Must hurry,' and flapped into the bathroom. Whence tumbled, like a brook running over rocks, the sounds of spluttering in cold water.

The toings and froings of her going passed me by. I sat at

the kitchen table and consumed my customary breakfast – the limited nutritional value provided by nicotine and coffee. It's a commencement to the day which gives one an appetite for anything. It precludes nothing; it leaves one with a blessed blankness – a state I had wrought to a well-nigh mystical perfection when I had been 'on the boards' ha ha. In a corner with a can of lager, prior to performance, I had been able to induce in myself an Eastern emptiness, resulting in an acting style so dull it had been called Brandoesque.

'I'll see you this evening,' Eth with the mandatory hushedness of a two-minute call. She left me all alone to step out on to there, where a vicious audience waited for my unlearnt lines. I felt the old dread of being pinioned on stage by silver shafts of light. With no words, no fucking words, trying to retch up pre-digested words. Gasping air up from inside myself, and the stalls full of Willy's playmates, dangerous men all, becoming dissatisfied as I gagged on silence. I couldn't retire; I was condemned publicly to stick on this unforthcoming vomit.

I extracted myself from the kitchen. It was a delicate operation, like tweezing a splinter from a swollen toe. I coaxed myself gradually out of doors and stood on the street and glanced in both directions, to see it extending with horrifying banality on either side of me. It reminded me of a ribbon of liquorice extended to the utmost of its elasticity in a child's hands. I turned rightwards along this friable strip.

Then left, then left again; a tightrope tremble of four hundred yards and I was there. I found myself staring at a blank house. It told me little. It had the shabby look of a place that was only ever temporarily tenanted. Lace curtains stagnated behind the windows, washed or unwashed into greyness. The front door was painted vanilla – perhaps the undercoat of a decoration that was never finished. There were three doorbells – all anonymous. I tried to remember what it was that reputedly came in threes

– troubles? fates? triplets? No matter. Start at the bottom and work up. I rang the lowest and waited.

I was listening for a click or a rattle or a cough. At length I heard a soft-slipper shuffle coming down the hall; the feet of someone old, dragging. Then a chain was put up by uncertain hands and the door opened eight or so inches. I saw a slice of a man in grubby white shirt and braces. His trousers were coal-grey, loose and wrinkled, like the skin of an ageing elephant.

'What is it?' An irascible voice, bubbling through phlegm-ridden lungs. A man not wanting or expecting callers.

'I've come to see someone. A girl who lives here.'

'Which one?'

I issued the official description. I was hoping that she might have owed rent, that this partial person might be excited by the sniff of money – assuming that he was the landlord anyway.

'Not here,' he said. 'Gone away.'

The door began to close. I jammed my foot in with a salesman's speed and suavity. 'If I'm taking up your time,' I assured him, 'I'll see it's made up to you.' It sounded over-eager, not indirect enough, but it worked. As slowly as a clam the door eased open.

'She went out a week last Saturday. She hasn't been back since.' The clack and suck of ill-fitting dentures as he spoke. His bifocals were held together with Elastoplast – the makeshift addenda to a decaying face. I could see yellow flecks of dandruff on his shoulders, although he was nearly bald.

'Can I have a look round her room?'

He squinted at me, the bright haze of daylight from the street pressing on his eyeballs. 'You're not a whore and you're not a nigger.' A compromise between a laugh and a cough – call it a caugh – hacked through his throat. 'You can have it.'

I shook my head. 'I don't want it. I just want to look

round.' I pulled out the soothing, folding stuff. It felt fresh and sensuous, full of the promise of things it could become. The landlord's liver-spotted fingers closed slowly round a tenner, like the tired hand of a swimmer on a lifebelt. A submarine hand. And the form of his thin legs was discernible against the back of his trousers as he bent forward striving up the staircase.

He reached the top and halted. From a gaoler's ring of keys he selected one and manipulated it in a Yale lock, outwitting the stubborn door with twists and tugs. Then he stepped back and showed me a musty, dusty room.

'What did you know about her?' I asked.

'Nothing.' Already he had begun negotiating his way down the staircase with the speculative progress of an invalid, clutching the banister and tentative toes testing the height of each step. 'I never ask questions as long as I'm paid on time.'

'How long had she been here?'

'Five weeks. Always take the rent a month in advance. Don't get caught out.' This last was delivered half as an account of his method and half as a piece of advice.

'Her real name? She must have signed a contract.'

'A verbal agreement's good enough for me. A verbal agreement plus cash. Talk to Nina.' The old man's finger shaking at the ceiling. 'Flat above.' And he carefully resumed his downward journey.

I looked round the room. The sheets were still rumpled on the bed, static like polluted snowdrifts in the city. There was a wardrobe and a chest of drawers with a mirror propped on it and a set of shelves in a recess with four books stacked sloppily on the highest.

I began in the wardrobe. Blouses and skirts and a couple of coats suspended on the hangers, sufficient to fill a medium-sized suitcase, no more. They were of a better quality than you might have expected – some of them. What was good was worn and what was new was cheap. I ran them along the rail, searching for a name tag – an identifying label sewn in. And I didn't find one; only a rectangle in the collar of a dress where the stiching had been carefully snipped out. It was though she had struggled meticulously to erase herself from history, to live out a shadowed existence with a thin alias between herself and the world. There was no handle to her, nothing I could get a grip on.

The chest of drawers likewise revealed nothing. Some items distinctly for professional use. The sort of underwear advertised in the personal columns of the Sunday news-papers. A second skin to slip into, for the benefit of the paying customer not satisfied with the first; and flesh-coloured appurtenances for those not satisfied with the flesh. Supplied by Uncle Willy, no doubt. As a perk.

Two nondescript thrillers slouched on the bookshelf, next to them an American edition of *The Turn of the Screw*, disguised as a nondescript thriller. The front cover showed a man with red fingernails and a green face wearing a top hat. 'The most chilling story ever told!' was captioned in gore-dripping capitals. A morroco-bound Bible lay flat beside it – the true touch for sentimentalists. I supposed bitterly that it had been given her by her parents, and I knew that if it had ever had a dedicatory inscription that would have been removed. I flicked it open and found the first page gone; only a ragged stump of paper buried in the binding.

I sat down on the edge of the bed. In this nameless room. In front of me dizzy-dotted patterning climbed the wall, torn at top and bottom. It had turned out to be so different from the room of my imaginings – that pink and fluffy place with its child atrophied in innocence. The victim I had prepared in my mind to go like a lamb to the slaughter. And I had sent her as far as the tube station, fantastically purified for sacrifice, leaving behind not this venal, dandruffed landlord but the inexorable justice of a maternal instinct. That would have been a different story. Nothing to do now but talk to Nina. I left the room with its door significantly ajar and ascended a further flight of steps – uncarpeted, with a wide path of darker wood down the middle, marking where a carpet had once been. I made it to the final landing. The day was draining on to it through a moth-spattered skylight. I knocked on this, the third door, and heard a whimper from within. I took it to be a snivelled response and entered.

A girl with a complexion the colour of congealed candle wax shivered in a rocking chair by the window. Black pin-head pupils floated in her soupy eyes. She was wrapped in a white sheet printed with pale pansies; heads, hands and feet poking out of it. She made me think of an insect camouflaged on a charred tree, looking like a twig that would disintegrate ashily on a breeze. Her hand went up to pinch the bridge of her nose and the sheet slid off her stick-like arm, to reveal track marks along the central veins, like the identations left by spiked running shoes. She sniffed drily, compulsively.

'You must be Nina,' I said.

'Nina, Tina, Sheena, Ribena.' A voice like fallen leaves rustling. 'We don't have names here. Not names that matter. We're just this one or that one. We buy and we sell.'

'Karen. Who lived below you. What was her name?'

'Karen. Sharon. Nobody ever lived below lived me.' Self-indulgence seemed to be the penultimate luxury of such a condition; a winding-sheet the last.

'What was her real name?' I was firing the question yet again, this time at a target so thin it seemed like aiming at a piece of paper edge on.

'The girl's frightened,' said Nina. Her unfocused eyes flitted over the windowpane's smeared surface. 'She tells me things. Things she doesn't want anyone else to know. I'm her best friend, see? I can't give away secrets.' A queasy selfishness slid through her tone. She was protecting whatever it was that made her important for these few moments.

I wondered whether I should tell her Karen was dead and

63

slash away her signficance with a stroke. Decided not to. It would only have made her the unreliable guardian of another secret.

'But I've got her passport. I took it from her room last week. I'm keeping it till she gets back. And I've got other documents. Papers proving – '

'Proving what?'

'What her real name is.' Her lips curled back in silent, sarcastic laughter. 'I can't let you see them, though. I'm her best friend and I couldn't do that.' A dry, compulsive sniff. 'Nobody gives things away here.'

'No,' I assented. 'It wouldn't be right.'

'But we sell things. She would understand if I sold them.'

'How much?'

'Money's no use to me. You get me some good smack. Bring some good smack and I'll give you her passport, her diary – '

'Her diary?'

'She's a nice girl. She keeps a diary. She must have been well brought up. I'll give you everything. I'll let you fuck me if you like.'

'Thanks.'

'I do it all the time.'

'Thanks,' I said again, and turned to go.

'Who are you, by the way?' Her voice chased after me, like an autumn leaf pursuing a pedestrian's ankles.

'I'm just a dealer,' I said. 'I'll get you some smack.'

And so I hurried to see Charlie. I had a sense that Nina's time was limited, as though she had been merely a ghost appearing to meet me in an attic, or a phantom granted a few hours before fading back into the fireplace. Certainly she seemed unreliable, intangible almost; she was probably lying about the diary. But she was going to have to give me something to get what she wanted.

I dived into the tubes, like an insect penetrating beneath the city's skin, burrowing into these black veins and cellular trains. The carriages clashed and clattered and the passengers sat stiff and solid in their seats, their hands folded in their laps. Their faces and postures reminded me of small gods lined round the walls of a shrine. They looked greedy for petty gifts, little tributes. Their wooden limbs shifted slowly at stations, carrying their bodies like bundles to the platform. More bodies implacably replaced them.

I tangled with them: at the exits and the entrances, where the inrush and the outrush foamed against each other; floating up the escalators, prodded by parcels; and at the gate, where the ticket-collector snapped tickets under his flat hand. And beyond there the surge flowed freely, staining the street like corpuscles from a gash.

I stopped by a newsvendor's deserted pitch and lit a cigarette, afflicted by giddiness as the city bled about me. Rose-coloured patches scarred on my retinas as I blinked, as when having stared at a burning bulb for too long. I tried to work out why this sudden fit of paranoia had beset me. It might have been nothing more complex than last night's whisky, with its afterpoisons still dancing a jittery conga round my skull. But, more likely, it was caused by the well-nigh unbelievable fact that I was involved in a murder; and, consequently, I was attributing a psychopathic mask to everyone.

Yes; I, Angelo, of all people, was tracking down a killer. Yet, in spite of the precise nature of this quest, I hadn't quite settled in my mind that anyone was particularly to blame. I suppose Eth held 'male violence' responsible. I couldn't even be that specific, though. I put it down to a nastiness in the air – a more pervasive cousin of the party spirit. I wondered how I could catch it.

I sucked hard on my cigarette and told myself to be normal, to start walking – which nearly everybody can and does do. As easy as falling off a log and very therapeutic. I made it to Charlie's flat, where I spoke first to a plastic, slatted box containing Charlie's voice. Buzz, click, and the door twitched open. Charlie was sitting impassive in his armchair, contemplating the blue-grey blossoms spreading from the tip of a long joint. They dissolved on the air like a magician's paper flowers. He was wearing a black velvet coat, unbuttoned and a lime-green shirt.

'Can you,' I asked, 'produce some smack out of nowhere?'

'No,' he said. 'How much do you want?'

'Twenty quids' worth, maybe.'

'You don't want that stuff.' Charlie shook his head; a moral decisiveness. 'You don't want to do that.'

'It's not for me. It's for someone else. She's an addict. She's practically dead anyway.'

'You're going to give her an extra push?'

'One further down the line. To stop the shivers.'

'Explain.'

I explained, beginning with Eth's intervention in my placid existence and continuing right to the end – or the middle, or wherever the hell I was – missing out nothing except what I had forgotten and the passage I was afraid might offend him – namely, Nicola's obscure infidelity. Left as a lacuna. Charlie picked at the narrative like someone inspecting a carpet. I think he was looking for severed threads.

'It's not good,' he said. 'It's best to ignore these things.'

'I can't do that now. Not now Willy's in on it. Willy and his money.'

'I don't like smack.' Oh! the connoisseur's eclecticism! 'The people who deal in it are a different class. Coke, dope – that's you and me – the degenerate middle class. But heroin – that's chaps in flash cars and flash suits carving each other up. And there's another problem. If they think you want it for yourself they won't let you go. They're as pushy as any other sort of salesmen. If they think you're going to deal in it, then you're cutting in on their market. Which is even worse for you.'

'You must know someone. I'll handle it.' I felt as desperate as a man in a quicksand promising to turn cartwheels.

'Supposing you get some. Supposing you take it to Nina and she tells you the girl's name. What then?'

'Eth stops pestering me. For a day or two. Willy gets a return on his investment.'

'But you're no nearer the truth.'

'That elusive quantity.'

'Leave well alone. Everything's very tidy as it is. Finding things out doesn't make for more tidiness. It just means there are more loose ends.'

'Aren't you,' I asked, 'just the least bit inquisitive? The fact of someone being murdered may be utterly banal nowadays. But someone turning up to buy the body the next day? Isn't that a little out of the ordinary?'

'It's odd. And it still doesn't interest me.'

It was typical of Charlie, of course, to consider a curiosity commonplace and a commonplace curious. He could stare at a shoelace for hours; but tell him that the shoe it was attached to once belonged to King Herod and he would be sure to ignore it. All the same, I found this apathy disconcerting. It seemed almost to be a deliberate reproduction of a fog, like dry ice. A cold, synthetic miasma. I said –

'What did happen that night?'

Charlie chuckled a disbelieving chuckle, as of someone who could take offence but who was too amused or too secure to bother. 'Inquisitiveness and suspicion,' he meditated audibly, 'are very close. You discover the truth's hidden then you imagine people are trying to hide it. It's not healthy – this addiction to truth.' In his bizarre coat with its ruffed collar he had the emaciated, impoverished air of a minor poet trying to be romantic. 'Do you suspect me?'

'A passing cloud,' I told him. 'I suspect you of nothing worse than idleness.' That, and a mind unduly relaxed; a smoke-screened mind, perceiving the world beyond like an aquarium full of silent swimmers.

'Angelo, my son, I suspect you of naïvety. If you blunder about in the jungle you're going to disturb the snakes.

Murder, prostitution, heroin – you can't get antidotes to the men who deal in those. Poke them with a stick and they'll bite you fucking hard. At least.'

'I've disturbed them already.' I realised sharply that Charlie was receding, like a man backing over a cliff in order to avoid a bore. He was about to plummet irretrievably down the chasm of his own consciousness. I needed a dramatic ruse to snatch him back. 'Do you know what's worse than being tortured for information you have?'

'No.' He answered as though it were of no more importance than a riddle.

'Being tortured for information you don't have.' A Wildean resonance there. It might appeal. 'I've got to know something they don't. Then I can negotiate surrender terms. Should the need arise.'

'Point taken,' said Charlie, too abruptly. I wondered if he'd agreed simply to stop me arguing. 'I'll try Mick.'

He rang Mick and we waited. Charlie made an omelette and I made a trip to the off-licence. We played three reckless games of chess, our pieces hurtling across the board in ambitious, lonesome missions. A crippled knight hopping from side to side. An insulted queen ensnared by lesser beings. The old king hobbling Learishly as twinned rooks alloted him his fate. And pawns scattered leaderless on the field.

Charlie put on a Doors album and we listened to Jim Morrison's sea-blue voice, crashing on the beach, casting up its strange cargo. Outside, brightness and gloom alternated. It had been one of those days when a low, dishwater sky had kept slipping under the sun before draining away again. Bringing no rain. And we listened to more records. Cans accumulated around us like the turrets of a derelict castle; roaches like whitened bones stubbed in a saucer.

'How's Nicola?' I enquired at one point.

'In love,' said Charlie. 'With a schoolteacher. They stare into each other's eyes and talk about the problems of inner city comprehensives. She's become a very concerned and sincere person.'

'Sex?' Tactless of me, but such matters are always intriguing.

'I don't think so. They both wear dungarees.'

'Rules sex out almost completely.'

'Convenient when decorating the home though.'

'I meant, what sex is the schoolteacher?'

'Difficult to be sure,' said Charlie. 'Probably whatever it feels it should be.'

'Does it have a name? That could be a clue.'

'She refers to it as Fran.'

'Ah.'

We carried on waiting – time ticking like an irritation for me, but each tick probably a series of spasms for Nina. Charlie told me what he knew about Mick. A Glaswegian, it was rumoured that he had been in the IRA, but had been expelled after exhibiting an enthusiasm which was deemed undisciplined. He had come to London – where he had announced himself by stabbing a night club bouncer five times in the stomach. The management, impressed by his business-like manner, took him on as a replacement and he repaid them by terrorising the patrons until the establishment was nearly bankrupt. But, by all accounts, his employers were too frightened of him to try to fire him. He finally left of his own volition, on the grounds that the work was no longer sufficiently challenging for a man of his proven ability.

He lived for a time by robbing robbers – a genus of crime he chose on the reasonable assumption that it would never be reported to the police. Having been dissuaded from this by several silver-tongued crowbars, he retired to the gentle pastures of drug dealing.

'In short,' Charlie concluded, 'he's fucking bad news.'

The entry phone's bell sounded, and a cement mixer voice ground after it. Charlie got up and pressed the button. And Mick lurched in with a skewed stride – the legacy of a shattered kneecap. A black beard sprouting out of his cratered face. He had a sniper's screwed-up, accurate eyes, and a low forehead with greasy hair stuck over it, like straw trampled into the mud. And I had seen him before (had I not?) across the room at Charlie's party; he had been standing atilt next to his host, and his shrewd features had been creased by puzzlement.

'It's a lot of stairs for twenty-five fucking quid,' he said.

'Twenty,' I corrected.

'Thirty-seven. I fucking counted them.'

'Twenty pounds.' Polite but firm. A figure was specified.

'Charlie said twenty quids' worth. That'll cost you twenty-five.'

9

I opened Nina's door without knocking, feeling that politeness would have been a disservice both to the general ambience and to my temporary function. Beyond the door an intermittent darkness hung, like smoke over a doused fire. The girl's shape stirred and subsided like a sheet of newspaper in a draught. She was still by the window.

'I'm back,' I announced with cheerful superfluity, as though from a merely domestic shopping trip. 'Where's the light switch?'

'On your right.'

A globe of yellowness spawned in the room. It smeared across Nina's face; her lips also – which were tugged upwards into a fixed grin by a bruise. Her skin was distorted like canvas nailed up, and her left eyebrow was squashed, split and swollen over its eye. From cheekbone to jaw the flesh was roughed, ridged and broken. It reminded me of an old, encrusted oyster shell.

'You won't give me that stuff now.' Her voice squeezed out in ugly lumps, like undigested food regurgitated slowly down the chin. 'Not now I haven't got it. What you wanted.'

'What happened?'

'Nothing that hasn't happened here before.'

With the sheet wrapped round her I had the impression that I was speaking to a head without a body – a head floating mutilated just above a rocking chair. 'Where is this "here"?' I asked. 'The here you keep referring to?'

'Shadowland. Karen calls it Shadowland. She says it's like in a poem where people are waiting for a boat. They're dead but they haven't been buried. They suffer but they're not alive.'

'Who was it?'

'I don't know. There were two of them. They weren't pimps. When pimps do it they don't want to damage you. They beat you with wet towels so they don't mark you. Or they put you in a bath full of spiders. Willy's done that to me but he's never damaged me.'

'What were they like?'

Her fingers crept out from under the sheet like worms and wriggled on her knee.

'I could use some of that stuff. I'll pay you for it when I can. When I'm working again.'

I was leaning against the wall. The breadth of my shoulders spread against the plaster. In a position of power, drinking in her vulnerability, as though blood were being pumped straight out of her body and into mine. Or as though I was sucking straight on a wound of hers. Warmth spurting in the throat.

'Will it help you remember?' A stupid, temporising question.

'It always helps.'

71

'Go ahead then.' I tossed her the powder packet. It reminded me of the sachets of salt provided in fast food restaurants; of convenience food, anyway. Her hand clutched out for it like a boat-hook. She unwrapped it with shaky carefulness.

'Until I was seventeen I thought you had to inject this. Boiling needles and all that crap. They try to make you think it's worse than it is. Then they make it worse than it is by telling you things like that. It's very clean really. Very easy.'

'Sure,' I said.

'Pass me that mirror.'

It was a hand-mirror with a pink, plastic frame, its cheap surface bending reflections like an oil-filmed, stagnant pool. I walked round the bed and handed it to her and watched her snorting – like an alcoholic striving not to spill a drop on some trembling Sunday morning. The nerve-ridden body refusing to acquiesce to its own desires when its whole existence has become a tic. Nina's nostrils fluttered like a fly's sprayed wings, before she threw her head back with the movement of a swimmer flicking water out of her hair.

I took the mirror and what was left of the heroin from her relaxed hands. And then myself sitting on the corner of her bed, leaning forward to catch her fractured voice. I felt like a priest in a confessional or a voyeur at a peep-hole. Examining corruption from my privacy.

'What were they like?' I asked again.

It took me well into the night to assemble Nina's story. Incoherencies, fantasies, irrelevances, contradictions and repetitions – they tumbled out as though a rubbish skip were being emptied. And I was attempting to collate, clean and assemble some shattered object from this wreckage, and she was all the while tipping more garbage on to the sliding pyramid.

'She's not one of us,' said Nina. 'She's not a scrubber. She didn't know anything when she started. She'd have someone down in her room and he'd want her to do something and she'd have to come up here to ask me what he meant. It used to make me laugh.' A laugh. To show me what a laugh was. 'She doesn't mind about the work though.' Nina closed her eyes and spoke slowly; a charlatan's trance. 'She goes through it like a princess. Like it's a duty she's been given to do and she can't stop to think about it.

'That's something you get in prison, but I don't think she's been to prison. If she has it must have been by mistake. But she hasn't because she would have told me if she had. She tells me everything, with me being her only friend now.' The sentimentality of an illusion was seeping full like salt water into a sandcastle's moat. 'I'm the one she told her secret to.' She rocked back in her chair – the curator of gossip, hands folded in her lap. Three of her front teeth were freshly missing, as though she had abruptly acquired not the wisdom of age but the meanness of senility. I could imagine her cackling on a porch, discreetly dispensing malice.

'What secret?'

'She's escaped from something terrible.'

'What?' I demanded. 'Or haven't I paid enough yet?'

Sulky disappointment – as when a joke's narrator has delivered the punchline and the audience still waits. 'That is the secret. She's escaped from something. She's hiding.'

'Shit,' I said. 'You're shovelling me shit.' I had an urge to slap her pale, paper head, to see it swing from side to side on its thin, spring neck.

'She says she'll tell me one day. But you don't tell anybody anything until you trust them. Not here. Not where the whispers go round. When you're trying to get on the boat you don't have any friends. Not when a whisper's a ticket.'

'This whisper was a ticket?' Distastefully I pursued her vocabulary through the swell of its portentous metaphor.

73

'You can sell whispers. If they're worth something you can sell them. Or you can promise not to sell them and get even more. Then you can get out of here, like when you're buried. You can buy things and go places.'

'And what she knew was worth something?'

'That's why she won't tell me what it is. She's afraid I'll sell it and then they'll find her.'

'Who?'

'I don't know.' Nina was fading into a doze, nodding off – as though in lulling sunshine and the lapsed concentration of age. 'It would all have been in her diary. The one I was keeping for her.'

'You never read it?'

'No.' She tilted forward suddenly in her chair and held it balanced on the tips of its rockers, hunched as if she was about to launch all her fragility at me. 'I'm not very good with letters.'

'You mean,' I corrected, 'that you can't fucking read.' I was stuck with an illiterate Sybil, casting books unread into the fire.

'Those two this afternoon kept asking me if I'd read it. They wouldn't believe me when I told them I hadn't. They didn't believe why not. They just kept hitting me. And the big one with his cigar.' She thrust a foot at me. Red-black blisters bubbled on it bigger than sixpences. 'Stubbing it out and then lighting it again. He was a bleeding sadist.'

I recognised him gradually: a familiarity approaching into precision, like the first symptoms of a repeating dream. The same slow, shaven figure lumbering through Nina's shredded recollection as had lumbered into Charlie's flat. He had declared himself by administering a beating. Without preliminary explanation. His stony fists doing their work automatically, as though they were unavoidably a machine for pounding people, of which he was the incidental operator – a divine justice descending immutable, implacable, in process. His graven face stared down at the snapped twig-figure on the floor and his slab-like foot swung forward for a kick. He uttered the single word – 'Slag.'

'The other sod looked about nineteen. He still had spots and he stank of aftershave. The sort who can't get an erection and pretends it's your fault. Start fiddling about with themselves and swearing at you at the same time. He started going through my things. Picking them up with his fingers like he could hardly bear to touch them.'

His virgin hands fiddling with unidentified objects. Dipping into the drawers and pulling out plastic novelties. Things that aroused suspicions and maybe more. Repelled, perhaps, by his own fascination, whilst searching for the passport and the diary. Those chrysalid whispers that never fluttered into words.

'I hadn't really hidden them so he found them nearly right away. They waved them at me like they'd proved I'd done something and they said they'd keep burning me until I told them I'd read them.'

'Why did they stop?'

'I don't know. They may have got bored. I've had plenty like that. You groan and scream a bit and tell them how strong they are and they soon get fed up.'

'And then they went away?'

They had gone away. I saw them leaving, the younger one going first with the queasy fanaticism of an altar boy in the presence of his bishop. Having officiated in an apprentice's capacity at this crippling sacrament, he hoped he had pleased. I guessed he was intoxicated with his initiation into purple-shadowed, gold-glimmering ceremony. And the older one, anti-mysterious, believed only in the efficacy of thuggery – of hitting people with his hands. His granite thighs grinding their plod from horizontal to vertical.

I decided that it was time to follow and collected the remaining heroin. There was nothing further to be learnt or purchased.

'Let me keep it. Please.'

'Nothing for nothing,' I said. 'You promised and you didn't deliver.'

'Her real name,' she peaded 'Part of it.'

'Go on.'

'Linda.'

A fact as useless to me as the stuff I exchanged it for.

Dawn was already weakly in the sky when I left; the colour of veal as night's black blood drained off. I walked home, to find that Eth had usurped my bed again. An untimorous Goldilocks browbeating the bears.

She stirred as – like a puppet putting itself away – I folded my limbs to the floor. Mutters from untidily recumbent Eth, no doubt taking leave of some interlocutor she had met in sleep's chance salon. I listened to the gutteral bye-byes of somnolent conversations as she unravelled herself to the gate where wakefulness began –

'Where've you been?'

'Shagging sheep,' I replied, my forehead rested on a crooked arm. 'Mopsy, Flopsy, Dropsy, Popsy, Poxy, Syphilis and Death.'

'Pardon?' She blinked emergently at this oddity of consciousness.

'I'm counting them. The ones I shagged.'

'What the fuck are you talking about?' Blurred words like a tape running slow.

'I'm trying to say, in my obscure little way, that I'd like to sleep.'

'You can do that later. I'll make some coffee and you can tell me what you've found out.' Her drowsy body slipped out of bed with the depressing momentum of a corpse tipped down the side of a mass grave.

I returned from the kitchen with a partial, yawning liveliness. And I told her my story, words cracking dry like nutshell shards in the throat. It's strange how simply being awake too long induces thirst – as though life were a two handed operation wringing avidly, and me a window leather in its rotating hands, divulging murky drops. The drop, drop, drop of dirty water as I recited all so far to happen. Concluded with the final twist.

'Now we know,' said Eth.

'What do we know?' I countered. 'Except that we know nothing?'

'That we started at the wrong end. We cherched la femme when we should have been cherching le man. The man who bought the body. He's obviously the one who killed her.'

'It's not obvious to me.'

'He had the motive. She was in a position to blackmail him so he killed her. Then he found out where she'd been living and recovered the diary.'

'If the diary ever existed. If it wasn't just a melodrama transferred straight from television to Nina's enfeebled imagination. An excerpt from an American crime series.'

'And he was sure the body was at Charlie's flat. He couldn't have known that unless he'd killed her himself.'

'Yes he could,' I said.

'How?'

'Let's suppose he had killed her. I don't for a minute think he did – for a start, anyone over fifty at that party would have been as conspicuous as a drunk at a mullah's funeral. It's not as if he's an ageing hippy even. But supposing he had sneaked in and done the deed. He comes back for the body the next morning. We don't know why he wants it – it's not the sort of thing that's useful around the home. And he has no guarantee that the place isn't already crawling with police. He doesn't know that Charlie hasn't called them.' I placed a pause swaying like a rope bridge across my speculations. And then – 'Unless . . .'

'Unless what?' The heroine, suspended by suspense, laid claim to another episode.

'Unless Charlie had been in touch with him.'

That doubt which had been sewn under my skin and didn't belong there: it was like an alien impregnation, an

77

organism doubling its size hour by hour. I feared that it would spread and swell until it split me open. It was a doubt about the only principle I maybe, casually and generally imperceptibly, believed in – the abstract, dissolvable connection of friendship. I suspected that Charlie – like Eth, but perhaps more subtly – had fucked me around.

I told Eth a story. Something with gaps in it. A tapestry with faces and motivations eaten out by moths, so that completion was a matter of guesswork; of leaping chasms at their narrowest points; of hurtling over dizzying depths of air from one sandy foothold to another. I said –

'We've swapped Karen for Linda.' Like changing currency at a border. Entering a new territory with a different coinage. 'So we'll call her Linda from now on. And we'll have to say that somebody wanted her dead – that we're dealing with a conspiracy and not an untidy, splattering outburst of frustration. Not beer and lust at a party boiling someone from the inside. Although,' I added, with my mind skimming over the possibilities like a helicopter hedge-hopping, 'we're all familiar with that raging, insulted hunger. That scarlet delusion when a room full of people smells like an abattoir. You see them loitering like sides of meat swaying on hooks. And some are hot and some are cold and you can smell the hot ones. And you have this yearning to burrow your hand into an open stomach and unwind its guts.'

Pause. Eth blanched as though her blood had taken the precaution of fleeing. And she was frightened and thinking, in this hallucinatory dawn having slipped from sleep's pale faces to these more material gibberings. No doubt she was rerunning inside her film-vault skull those movies in which the kindly psychopath spares his pursuers any further labour by the abbreviating device of unveiling himself in a series of obsessional outpourings. ('They never cleaned their fingernails . . . My mother, she used to lock me in a cupboard if I didn't clean my fingernails . . . It was

78

so dark . . . My God! When I saw how dirty their fingernails were . . .') No, no, sister; I may be odd, but it wasn't me. Tee hee.

'I think this man – the anonymous one – let's call him the stone man – had a motive for arranging the girl's demise. He sounds to me, above all, a respectable fellow. That's to say, the type who would use a prostitute. He probably had some way of explaining the fact that he fucked her to himself – some solid, sentimental understanding of it. I can imagine him convincing himself that he would one day rescue her from her sordid life. Or, even worse, that he loved her. Some bourgeois banality transmogrified into a glorious, worthy passion.

'Then, one afternoon, as he was mantling his lithic body for the world, doing it with the cumbersome tidiness he always did it with, Linda suddenly perceived his essential respectability. She realised that he had a wife and children and that precious thing known as "standing in the community". She realised, moreover, that those were assets he could be made to pay for and she named a price. The stone man, our solid, sentimental citizen, was horrified. He instantly understood that he had been screwing something as uncomplicated and as incomprehensible as meanness. He shouted at her, he slapped her and he drove her away.

'And as he drives his estate car – that very tangible symbol of family life, bought for the sake of the holiday luggage or the dog in the back – his thoughts gurgle like a whirlpool round the girl. How she deceived him, how she sucked him in. He's furious because he was stupid enough to squeeze out his cream topping love on that avaricious little bitch. He sees it as a waste – a fraudulent diminution of his resources, like the money he's already spent on her. And he remembers the lies he had to tell his restless wife as she took turns around the lounge. And his lies strike him as sores that have to be guarded because if they're picked or probed they may become ineradicable infections. And he speculates on the confusion that that girl could stir into his life – like when a malicious child's switched the salt with the sugar. He has a foretaste of his whole existence as a nauseating dinner that he's going to have to eat course by course, day after day.

'So he drives to his local and orders a large Scotch and soda. Then he has another and another. And the more he drinks the more surely he begins to believe in something which often appears with a hazy sort of clarity to men in his condition. He becomes convinced that a certain solidarity exists between all males everywhere and that therefore he can tell the barman, or whoever's sitting next to him, or some casual semi-stranger, the circumstances of his predicament. And he's convinced, too, that this random man will sympathise absolutely.

'That's all he wants: sympathy. He wants someone who'll tell him that the same thing happened to him not so long ago and not to worry because it soon blew over and these silly cows always try to frighten you and so on. But that's not what he gets because he talks to the wrong man. He talks to someone who's even more astute than Linda at trading on frightened respectability. Someone who, we know, used to make his living out of the fact that the middle class hates a fuss.

'That's why the night club owners employed Mick. They wanted a bouncer because bouncers stop that unpleasantness known as fuss occurring. And they kept him on when they thought that to get rid of him would cause even more fuss. So when Mick was approached by the stone man he knew exactly how to behave. He exaggerated the difficulties. He emphasised the dangers. It's as though he were a miner who had discovered a seam. He drilled along the cracks. He planted explosive in the crevices. He chipped and tunnelled and the stone man crumbled. He agreed to pay Mick to kill the girl.

'From that moment it was simple and inevitable. Mick set about his work. He collaborated with Nicola and Charlie.

They settled the time and the place and Nicola was deputed to lure the girl there. It was no more difficult than reeling in a hooked fish. And when the circumstances seemed propitious they slipped the fish off the hook and battered its head on a rock. The fish gasped as much from surprise as breathlessness.

'The next morning Charlie rang the stone man. He told him to come and collect the proof of a job well done and to make the final payment. I'm sure, incidentally, that it wasn't the final payment. I'm sure respectability is still paying out for the promise of no further fuss.'

Eth had gone. She'd expressed herself entertained but not convinced by my improvisation. A disheartening response after I'd put so much effort into it – reminiscent of those auditions where the director requires you to sacrifice your dignity in some absurd verbal and physical contortion – 'Imagine you're Richard III applying for a job as a playground supervisor. Don't forget the disability' – and then doesn't offer you a part.

It was a matter of indifference at this strange hour. I plunged into bed with the careless enthusiasm of a conscripted soldier diving for cover. The freshly rumpled sheets were imbued with perfume and sweat, like mist hanging low over a still, morning sea. And I, sleeping in the imprint of another's body – it made me feel like an impersonator. I had the curious sense that a configuration of circumstance had wrenched me into the position of being nearly Eth.

Or, at the very least, of having undertaken her work – the search for her sister, which she had vehemently promised us both. It was as though, in fact, she were the will, the consciousness of the pursuit; and I had become merely its eyes, hands and feet: a plodding, brainless organism.

Watching my dumb feet splaying outwards on the pavement, walking an unhurried, dutiful pace in heavy boots, I drifted into a floating, superficial sleep. The kind of sun-spotted snooze that feels as if it's taken on a lilo, rocking on a ripple-ruffled surface with the prospect of wakefulness no nearer than the side of the swimming pool; until a disturber of the peace leaps feet first into the turquoise water and a splash like a coronet sprays suddenly up. That doorbell. Again.

Enrobed in olive green I rolled downstairs, sweet gravity providing all the pull. I opened the door to find a personable youth standing behind it. Personable: inoffensive without being charming. Short, blond hair and a complexion that could be described as volatile. Wearing a light brown suit. I would have assumed him to be a Mormon had it not been that he was holding, instead of a Bible, a box tied with string.

'It's full of food,' he told me. 'And things.'

'Ah,' I said. 'A sort of relief parcel. How kind.'

'It's not for you though.' The poor boy was flustered. A veritable cream-faced loon. 'It's for the old man across the road.'

'Then why,' I enquired, 'don't you give it him?'

'He's not answering. I was wondering if you could . . .?'

'Certainly,' I said, and licked my lips with ostentatious wolfishness. 'I'd be delighted.' I took the box in cradling arms. Spied silver-circle tin tops where its flaps failed to meet.

'There's a note for him in there,' added the boy. 'If you could just deliver it when he's in.' And he scurried away.

I carried the box into the kitchen and deposited it on the breadboard. Surveyed it. I concluded that it was capacious enough to contain up to twenty-four small cans of beer. But was probably full of baked beans. Best leave the string unsnipped and the disappointments unseen. What kind of monster could rob an old man of his meagre fare anyway?

Consequently, I was once more reclining in my deckchair when the bomb exploded. It went off with a surprisingly gentle crump, a soft and collapsing sound, and removed the furthest wall of my kitchen and most of the adjacent bathroom, projecting them into the garden beyond, where the imperturbable bath rested amid the grass like a baby hippopotamus. Plaster like shreds of soggy newspaper. Pipes hiccuping out bellyfuls of water. The contents of the concealing tins now spattered on the tiles above the breadboard. I adjudged them to have been mushy peas and carrots as they sludged downwards with the placidity of cold vomit. Indicating either gross insensitivty or Rabel-aisian humour on the part of my would-be, juvenile assassin..

I left my kitchen looking as though it had gorged itself and burst. Spewing its indigestible contents from every intestine and orifice. And went to the pub.

10

I was well into my fifth pint when Willy arrived – informed by some secret network not only of the explosion but also of my survival and whereabouts. He appeared with all the sinister good timing of an undertaker at a hospital bed, bought himself a Bloody Mary and joined me at the table. When he had settled himself he removed his fedora and perched it on one knee – as though his kneecap was the head of a dwarf who constantly accompanied him and was accorded the privilege of wearing his hat when he no longer required it.

'Mr Paris,' he announced, 'I am desolated to hear of your misfortune.'

'My landlord's going to be more desolated than either of us. He owns the goddamn place.'

'But you, meanwhile, are without a home. This is the cause of my sorrow.'

'You'll get over it,' I said. 'You'll get over it.'

'I fear not.' He took a sip of his drink. A line of tomato juice, like the sliver of a crimson moon, rimmed his lower lip. 'I fear that this morning's bang may have been intended as a warning to me. I have recently been reading your poet Shakespeare's most famous play – *Julius Caesar*. Its early sections are full of portents. I need not tell you what a portent is?'

' "When beggars die there are no comets seen; /The heavens themselves blaze forth the death of princes." '

'Exactly so. This bang foretells some tribulation for me. It is remarkable, is it not, how a mere bang can create within us such exact words and feelings. This uneasiness. This sense that something yet greater is about to happen.'

'I'm not superstitious,' I said, as if Willy had a heart like a coconut. Tap it and it was full of muted resonances.

'And you think I have a string of crocodile's teeth beneath my shirt and tie? This is not the case. But I can read the signs and a bomb is a very simple sign. I shall tell you precisely what it means.'

'Go on.' I prepared sceptically to discover what my kitchen's entrails patterned forth, having sorted through them in my own mind and found no heart.

'It means that in your search for Karen you have angered someone of importance. Someone whose anger will shortly be directed at me. You see how it is?'

'No.' I was irritated by his ponderous speech. It was like watching a liner drawing slowly to its berth. 'I don't.'

He sipped again noiselessly from his glass; then – 'When the girl disappeared, Mr Paris, three possibilities occurred to me. Firstly, that she had absconded of her own free will. Secondly, that she had been seduced by terms better than those I was providing. But, in either case, she would have taken her possessions with her – would she not? The third possibility, therefore, seemed most acceptable: that she had been abstracted by some violent and unforeseen incident.

'Whose interests would this serve? I asked myself; and the answer was clear. It would benefit a rival, a man attempting to make me look weak or foolish amongst my peers. It is common in this business to steal a piece of property not because the thief wants it, but to demonstrate that it can be stolen. You see, Mr Paris, how this erodes my standing?'

I nodded with more vigour than usual. Of course, I didn't fully understand his talk of reputation – not in the present context. But it seems there's no profession so shabby it doesn't have its pride.

'And I was the more injured,' he continued, 'because – of all my girls – he stole the one who was most special to me. She had, Mr Paris, both innocence and education attached to her.'

It was a fact which had evidently impressed him. We paused for a moment's semi-religious contemplation whilst it sank in. Then he resumed:

'But how was I to find my enemy if he would not show his face? How could I identify someone who functioned behind a mask? It became necessary to prod him.

'When you forced yourself to my attention, Mr Paris, I thought to myself "Here is an arrogant young man. He reflects on his own virtues so much that he has no time to consider his faults." It is impolite of me to say this, I know. But we are both familiar – are we not? – with the legend of the unicorn, which can only be ensnared by a mirror. It stands absorbed in its own image, contemplating what a fine unicorn it is, and the humble hunter approaches from behind with his net. You appreciate my comparison?'

'No,' I told him, 'not at all.'

'It seemed to me,' he went on, 'that if you believed yourself to be engaged upon some mysterious task of detection you would not realise that you were only Willy's

85

finger, administering a prod to my unknown enemy. This morning he responded to my prod.'

'And what does the bomb portend?'

'Ruthlessness. This is a ruthless man undoubtedly. He has a capacity for organisation. Patience also. This bomb foretells a time of great trouble for me.' A sigh. As of a man contemplating something he has endured before and must endure again. Relieving the dwarf of his hat in order to take him for a stroll, he observed – 'I see you enjoy your beer, Mr Paris. Permit me.'

I permitted him; and, whilst he was gone, I began to feel useless again. I blamed my adolescent angel and his bomb; not only had they demolished the arse-end of my home, they had also dented the theory which I had so fluently expounded to Eth. For, if this affair were no more than an infidelity gone sour – a frightened husband and a greedy whore – then he (the husband) would hardly have been likely to resort to such melodramatic measures. It would, truly, have been blowing things up out of all proportion.

No; the packaged device smacked of corporate crime. It belonged to Willy's world and it fitted with his theory. I had to concede the superiority of his case – even if the complacency with which he expressed it vexed me sore. And it was this complacency, I think (that and the six pints of beer), which made me do what I did next.

When he came back, carrying my glass as carefully as if it were full of noxious chemicals, I tried to shock him. In my best revelatory whisper I announced –

'Karen was murmured.'

He nodded like a psychiatrist soothing a dangerously deluded patient.

'Murmured,' he repeated.

'I'm sorry,' – scratching an eyebrow – 'murdered.'

'Murdered. Ah. This makes better sense. To say that she was murdered.'

'You're not surprised?'

'No,' he replied. 'This is the confirmation of my premonitions. Would you please reveal to me what you know of this murder.'

So I gave him the facts. The facts and nothing more. By themselves they looked as coherent as pins stuck in a blank board. And when I'd finished Willy stared into the depths of his upturned hat, holding it by the brim. Maybe he hoped that, in its gloomy basin, some face might take on form mouthing clandestine inspiration or a prophesy. Eventually he said –

'The Stone Age man, as you call him – he seems to signify a barbarity peculiar to your people. He is one of your ancestors, to whom I could address the words – "Get back in your cave, ape." Perhaps, one day, I shall have the opportunity to do so. But, whilst he and his tribe are rampaging, I think it will be expedient for you to be elswhere. As you have no home, I shall drive you to your young lady's residence.'

But, it being the middle of the day, we drove instead to Eth's place of work. Through the rectangular city, its geometry blocked out block by block. Buildings hewn in sharp-edged lumps, dusty dry in early autumn. A harsh sand-land, blowing like salt on the stump of a torn-out tongue. And there were people moving under this heat, as though intimidated by some metaphysical cruelty.

From the car's streaked window I saw a woman carrying two shopping bags, her shoulders hunched, like someone walking into a bitter wind. Washing suspended on the balconies of letterbox flats – the flags of tiny islands, all besieged. Another woman crouching over a child, deceiving its defences with double-handed slaps. A queue strung out from a bank like the tail of a twitching kite. Shuffling, shuffling, with the discreet feet of servants. A red bus, in every window the dulled faces of prisoners – unsure or too sure of their destination. The rhythms of persecution hauling them from one torment to another. I said to Willy –

'These people are no better than slaves.'

Behind his dark glasses his eyes shifted leftwards. He looked at me laterally without turning his head. 'Are you reiterating your accusations? The accusations your young lady made? I can provide many justifications.'

'No,' I said. 'It was a general observation.'

'Confine your observations to that on which you are qualified to speak.'

He swung round a corner with the swiftness of a man making no concessions to his passenger. His privilege, of course, to change direction. 'When my parents came to this country they believed – they sincerely, stupidly believed – its streets were paved with gold. That was the very phrase they used. They reassured each other with it as they embraced on the deck, wearing old coats. It was the phrase I saw in their eyes, hour by hour, growing brighter. We sailed from Lagos to Liverpool on the Elder Dempster line, now defunct. I recollect that the radiance in their pupils was scraped away a little on the train leaving Lime Street. As we settled in the carriage an adjacent family moved cautiously away. This was the first abuse my parents received in your homeland.' Willy stared steadily back, watching again his father's and mother's innocent humiliation. 'Tell me, Mr Paris, why do you adopt the forename Angelo?'

'A stage name,' I muttered. 'I used to act. It looks better on programmes.'

'I think you have a secret, Mr Paris.'

'Uh uh,' I assured him. 'No secrets.'

'I think your secret is that you are British. I think you try to hide this fact in order to be superior. You call these people slaves, and really you are one of them.'

'I'm as different as the next man.' Humour, brother. Humour.

'And the next man, in this instance, is me. Do not try to be black, Mr Paris. I would not respect that. I do not respect your young people when they inform us how much they admire our musicians or our cricketers. They are not doing it for us. They are doing it for themselves. They are doing it because they wish to escape the burden of being British. Your hippies who went to the East, your students who aspire to be working class, your punks who mimic the hairstyles of expropriated Indians – they are all playing in this charade. This desire to be oppressed. It is a desire I and my people have learned to do without.

'By way of illustration I shall tell you about the girl named Karen, or Linda. When she was brought to me I thought, "Here is a girl of good character. She is what is called respectable. Why is she doing this to herself?" I explained to her what her duties would be. I offered her the opportunity to leave. She did not flinch. She only enquired "Will there be men who want to hurt me?"

'I replied, "Fortunately, few. But often there will be men who wish to be hurt. Lords temporal and spiritual, judges, politicians, policemen, civil servants, captains of industry – they will come to you begging to be enchained and whipped." Yes, Mr Paris. The guardians of your empire come to the nigger's whore begging for a taste of the lash. They wish to strip and abase themselves before a black man's woman to atone for the guilt of being British.

'These revelations should not surprise you. You live in a masochistic culture and I shall tell you one more item to confirm this. When I informed the girl Karen that she would have to administer punishment she became perplexed. She confessed that she might be intimidated by such honourable rumps. She said it might seem more appropriate were the situations reversed. You see, Mr Paris, she was schooled to accept punishment. The prospect of giving it confused her. Do you think that therein is some clue as to why she inflicted that profession on herself?'

We drew up outside the Battersea Centre for Victims of Male Violence. I pointed to its signboard. Fresh white paint on pale blue. 'Some men,' I said, 'still like dishing it out.'

Down a snake-shaped path to the portals, my steps

winding along the serpent's back as though I were part of the oldest allegory in the world. And through these heavy doors to the functional foyer. It was long, flat and low – containing a slab of light and air; light and air that seemed to have stuck there like a slice of bread forgotten behind a fridge. On the wall facing me were paintings executed by the residents. Simian men swinging hammers in their hairy hands. Women with Munchian faces beneath lurid, vibrant skies. Here is the pain. See the pain. A simple, twisted sort of art. To my right was a girl in a pink housecoat, looking like a cherub in a primary school play. She was sweeping – managing her actions so that the angled-forward-angled arrangement of strokes always came to a point a yard ahead of her. But, strangely, the chequerboard floor had been scrubbed stringently clean and the focus of her sweeping was only an imaginary location where dirt or rubbish would have been. Had there been any. She swept conscientiously towards me across the spotlessness. And, without looking up, she said –

'You're a man.'

'How can you tell?'

'I listened to your footsteps. You shouldn't be here.'

'Why are you sweeping this floor?' I asked.

'We all help. We all do things. Now go away.'

'I've got mud on my shoes,' I told her. 'I'm going to walk across your floor.'

'It hasn't rained for weeks.'

'Gravel, then,' I suggested. 'Gravel from your path.'

'Please go away what do you want.' The two sentences ran together like messages issuing from a talking doll.

'I want to see Miss Spurgeon. Miz. Muz. Whatever.'

She raised her head and I saw that her eyes were covered by two flesh-coloured, circular dressings, as though two bulbous lumps of skin had been stuck there.

'I'll go and fetch her if you promise to wait outside. Do you promise?'

'Sure,' I growled graciously. 'That's no problem.'

I went back into the sunshine again. I found myself staring at a neat lawn, shaved into an Augustan tidiness. Half a dozen undistinguished trees sprouted from circles cut into turf. And beyond them was a sandstone wall; clogged up against it, the black, peaty earth of an empty flowerbed. I sensed the distinctive informality of an ingratiating institution – the disciplined soothing of a mental hospital, approaching like a nurse with a hypodermic and a smile.

'What are you doing here?'

'Eth!' I cried, not turning round. 'My darling Eth! I've been through so much since I last saw you and – do you know what? – it's all your fault.'

'Nothing to stop you going to the pub.'

'On the contrary. I was impelled there. Blown. Transported on billows, nay, pillows of smoke.'

'Stop farting about.'

Swivelled swiftly and stopped, like a stuttering Catherine wheel. Pressed my face up close to hers and opened my eyes wide, our noses almost touching. 'Boom!' I whispered, my hands measuring a radiating blast. 'Boom!'

'Boom?' queried Eth. Then sudden enlightenment. 'You've been made Chancellor of the Exchequer. You have to walk around saying "Boom!" '

'There was a bomb in my kitchen,' I hissed. 'Why do you think that was?'

'There was no room for it in the bedroom?'

'It wasn't in your fucking kitchen was it? "O absent presence, Ethel is not here." You're the absent cause *par excellence*. What philosophers have been searching for since ancient times. I ought to ring up Kant and tell him I've met the *primum mobile*.'

'You're not making sense, Angelo. You're raving.'

'You're never fucking there, are you? You started this ridiculous pursuit, but you've done no more than that. You merely put it in motion.' I seized hold of her lapels and lifted her towards me. The stop-start creak of stitching

91

tearing. 'I was nearly killed, dammit. And where were you? Why was it me who was nearly being killed? Why weren't you being killed? Why! Why! Damn you!'

I released Eth and sat down on the steps. I watched my right arm begin to shake. Soon it was twitching and flopping like an asphyxiating fish. The phenomenon known as delayed shock. Similar to a remark embedded in the memory, the full significance of which may become apparent only days later; a time-locked safe clicking open. As this arm, which was mine by all rights of possession, continued to dance to a different drum.

'I didn't think I'd ever say this,' said Eth, preening down her flustered pin-stripe jacket, 'but you need a drink. I've got a bottle of Scotch in my office.'

I was led subduedly down a pencil-line corridor. We passed a huge windowed room where two women sat, both knitting a pointlessly long scarf. Through the glass we could hear the needles' rapid clacking. I touched Eth's elbow.

'What are they doing?' I asked.

'I taught them how to knit,' she explained. 'A scarf was the easiest thing to start with. They began intending to wear them when they were finished, then it turned into a competition to see who could knit the longest. So now they'll never get finished.' She shrugged. 'I used to help them but I can't any more. It provokes jealousies. Accusations of favouritism.'

'Is this a madhouse?' It seemed a pertinent question.

'It's a cross-over point. We help victims of violence to face the real world again. Women who've suffered physically and mentally. It takes time.'

'The real world. That never-never land of sociologists. Perhaps this station is as real as anything.' It was a sententious remark. My brain, no doubt, had been affected by the emptiness of the place.

And on down we went, past the pathological knitters to Eth's office. It could have been a substantial room, but it was crowded into smallness by a desk, plastic orange stacking chairs, paper cups, documents and directories and a metal bookcase, volumes slumped aslant on the shelves. A two-tome work entitled *Incest Through the Ages* curiously consorting with an Enid Blyton paperback – *Fatty's Famous Tissue*. And inevitably there was a filing cabinet, from the bottom drawer of which Eth salvaged the promised bottle.

She inspected her array of paper cups, seeking a couple which evinced a measure of cleanliness. And eventually found them. They were filled up to a degree which I considered almost satisfactory. I helped myself to the fuller with a right hand which had resolved its movement to slow, subsiding jerks.

'Tell me about it,' said Eth.

I sipped and told her all.

When I'd finished I asked Eth a simple question – 'Who knows about the bombs? Who would use a bomb to kill someone?'

'A terrorist?' she ventured.

'A terrorist,' I repeated. 'Or an ex-terrorist. And who' – a butterfly wing's flicker trembling in my throat – 'have we encountered who fits into that category?'

'Mick?'

'Yes, indeed. Our wild man from the IRA.' A snippet from Charlie's biography and the safe door swung tantalisingly open. It was an inch ajar already. 'He was worried that I was getting too close. So he tried to kill me. Bingo.'

Eth reflectively tapped her cup against her teeth. 'Then why did he sell you the heroin? He must at least have guessed it was for Nina. He must have known it could only help you.'

'We'll find out why. Willy thinks it's another firm muscling in on his patch.' Jargon for authenticity. Or *au faiti*city. Being the subject of an assassination attempt confers on you a certain credibility. 'I'll ring him from your flat tonight and suggest that he talks to Mick.'

93

'Talks to him?' she queried with innocent surprise, as though I had promised nothing more forceful than tea and crumpets.

'Willy's a very persuasive talker. So many rhetorical resources.'

'Ah. That sort of talk.' Pause. 'And you said my flat.'

'I'm homeless, kid, don't forget. There's a hole in my home.'

'Then that'll make three,' Eth calculated. 'Nina's staying with me too.'

11

As soon as we arrived at Eth's, Nina scuttled to the bathroom to be sick. I rang directory enquiries to get the number of the Nile, and duly called it. I was calling desperately down the line, like a survivor in a night-time sea, chilled fingers to the rope, knowing that Mick was stumping the city with his stiffened leg, perambulating in ever-decreasing circles, drilling himself nearer this flat, penetrating the city with his corkscrew walk. Just walking, with the certainty frozen in his heart that keeping in motion would be sufficient to bring him to me.

'Willy,' I said, 'I've worked out who it had to be.'

A silence. Then – 'You claim to have worked it out? To have made a calculation? No more than this?'

'Yes. On the basis of facts.' I hoped that this might palliate the monstrosity of conjecture – the tenuousness of having only an emotional assurance of something. I had had a prevision of destiny I couldn't expect Willy to share.

'I shall find him,' he announced. 'And you will accompany me.' He said it as though he were doing nothing more momentous than illustrating a grammatical point.

I gave him Eth's address and then rang Charlie. The phone trilled in his flat like the sad, strange cry of a deserted bird. Trilling and trilling. It was typical of Charlie not to answer even if he was in. Irritate the bugger into submission, I told myself. And, at length, success.

'Hello.'

'Charles! My son!'

'Angelo, my child.'

'I want to see Mick again. Same as before. At your place. Can it be done?'

'I'll have to take a personal commission. I'm broke.'

'Granted. How soon?'

'A couple of hours anyway.'

'Love and kisses.'

'And you.'

I replaced the receiver and we began to wait. We were an awkward trinity, trying to co-exist. Nina sat rigidly in the middle of the sofa, her fingernails scraping on her flaking skin, attending to a constant itch, like a plough furrowing up a frosted field. I had never before seen her wearing anything other than her sheet, but now she wore a thin, blue blouse and a denim skirt. Eth busied herself without busying herself at anything, occupying herself with that tedious readjustment of props beloved of actors who lack the confidence to stand still. I drank slowly – another stock ruse for wasting time – keeping myself topped up. I was floating on that fragile cloud poised between a dizzying, orbital drunkenness and a disheartening descent to sobriety. I said to Eth –

'What's she doing here?'

Nina snivelled orphanically. Eth turned the flaming eyes of a protectress on me –

'I hope Willy enjoys your company more than I do. When you go off to do a man's work.'

'She's one of Willy's girls. She's not yours for the taking.'

'She is now.'

'I've got out, see?' said Nina. 'I've been transported. I knew it would come to some good – with you and the diary and those men. I knew it would work out.'

'All you need now,' I suggested, 'is your best friend back. Then your happiness would be truly complete.'

'Don't.' Eth snatched at the bottle which, once more, was tilting conveniently towards my glass. 'Sit there and shut up.'

'But,' I resumed, regaining mastery of the means of consumption, 'this is an unlikely eventuality. Indeed, to stress its unlikeliness, to give you some idea of how unlikely it is, I would describe it as requiring a precondition not known since our dear Lord and Saviour walked the earth. It would require a resurrection.'

'Jesus,' Eth whispered.

'Exactly.' I shook a cigarette at Nina. 'Your new friend appreciates my theological allusion. Your old friend appreciates nothing. She is dead. As a parrot.'

'Ignore him,' said Eth. 'He's drunk. He thinks he's being funny. Poor sod.'

'I feel it is my duty to warn you,' I went on, 'that the murderer is with us in this room. It is, of course, Ethel. Eth the Death, as she is known in the trade. Her attempts to silence me only confirm her guilt. But I must speak out. She is a notorious psychopath. She lures young women to her lair and butchers them savagely. I have come to warn you. You must flee. We must all flee.'

I slewed over in my armchair and slopped a thimbleful of whisky on my thigh. Leered mischievously at Eth who was staring at me with pallid fixity, all colour drained away except from those fabulous emerald eyes. They were fired like the twin talismans of some comic-strip deity.

'I don't care,' said Nina. 'I've gone away now. That man who came up the stairs and hit me won't come here. He won't come here.' She glanced up at Eth. 'I'd like to be killed by a woman.'

'That's great,' I muttered. 'That's great.'

Then we sat there saying nothing with the silence gaping at us like a wound: that special silence which descends after a row, when the proper thing to do is leave and close the door – but the temptation remains to stick another needle in regardless. Eth was breathing heavily, one arm stretched out along the mantelpiece, like a matador resting. I said to Nina –

'She's very touchy about her victims. All these sisters she protects who come to grief. She has to take responsibility for every one. Your rescuer. Who can't do a fucking thing. What's she going to do with you? What do you think she can do with you?'

'Shut up,' said Eth. 'We've had enough.'

'She can get me over. She can be my ticket on the ferry. The one Linda talked about before she got away.'

' "The longing hands reach to the further shore," ' I quoted glibly. And then the doorbell rang.

I sat in the front seat of Willy's habitual Mercedes. In the back were two men whom he introduced to me as Nelson and Frank. The one was surprisingly small and the other predictably large. Nelson – the small one – had a cheap suit on and sat with his arms entwined round each other like two wires. He had the attentive face and the eager restlessness of a child on an outing. Frank was in cement-smeared overalls and carried a metal toolbox on his knee. His features, in contrast, were battered and had the stupefied dignity of an oft-defeated boxer.

'Where are we going?' Willy asked.

I told him where Charlie lived. 'The man we want's going to be waiting for me,' I added. 'Or he should be.'

'You will explain more to me as we drive,' he decreed.

I went over my reasoning – what there was of it. As I tinkered with it, emphasised it, repeated it, it struck me somehow as a knot that wouldn't quite tighten. It seemed to keep slipping undone, refusing to tie together two things that had to be tied together. Occasionally Willy's eyes skidded from the road to me. When I began to go over it for the fourth time he said simply –

'It is sufficient.'

It had started raining whilst I had been in Eth's flat; raining on the dust-blown streets that had begun to prey on me like chapped lips. To begin with, the dust had merely commingled with the rain, washing suspended down the gutter streams like powdered milk failing to dissolve. By now, though, the dust had been lashed away and it had become difficult to remember or even to imagine what dryness was. The windscreen wipers swung right-left-right-left, swiping the drops sideways into rivulets. A pair of ceaseless policemen engaged on a futile patrol.

Willy began to expound in that measured, uninterruptable way of his. I settled myself down for another hefty dose of truth –

'The gentleman Nelson is my analyst and the gentleman Frank is my technician. These you consider glorified terms – terms which bestow too great a scientificity on a practice you consider vulgar thuggery. But permit me to use them. Think, Mr Paris, of the mechanism on which these gentlemen operate; then pass your judgement. I speak, of course, of the human body.

'The purpose of an analyst, my friend, is to break things down. To take them to bits. To undo them. I had cause to consult a dictionary recently, and there I discovered that the Greek word from which analysis derives can, in certain cases, mean death. This, then, is the task of the analyst in extreme instances – to put to death.

'But I need not tell you that a jeweller does not disassemble a watch with a hammer. He plucks out the tiny cogs and springs, employing steadiness of hand and sharpness of vision. He uses the faculties of a craftsman in setting about his destruction. This is how one should operate on the human body. Nelson, you will see, has a certain delicacy – an ability to prise open the gap between bone and socket – to discover the potentialities of neglected nerve endings. He works in such a way that the subject of his manipulations experiences new categories of pain.

'Pain, Mr Paris. You may never have observed it at close quarters but it is, I assure you, an entertainment. Like all great art, it forces in us a greater consciousness of our own mortality. To give you an example of this, Nelson was once required to blind a man. I recollect that his name was Cheshire. The business was carried out under sanitary conditions using a needle and a quantity of acid. As I watched I became acutely conscious of my own eyeballs. I felt their soft globes to be so ill-protected in my skull. I empathised with Mr Cheshire as the needle penetrated. My whole body felt as though it had been reduced to two globes suffering injection. My mouth opened of its own volition but did not form a scream.

'It is, you see, a question of aesthetics. The fact which I am trying to emphasise is that I had never been more totally awake. The achievement of this, Mr Paris, demands admirable accomplishments, both scientific and artistic.'

'And Frank?' I asked. 'What does he do?'

'He is, as I believe I told you, my technician. In a laboratory the circumstances must be appropriate before work is commenced. Frank ensures a placid and suitable circumstance.'

And, with flawless timing, Willy stopped the car. Perhaps he had paced out his soliloquy several times in rehearsal. The block of flats lay black beyond a brick wall like the huge flank of a whale. It was nearly midnight and only a few dribbles of light showed, leaking from behind closed curtains. Harpoon wounds.

'He's a hard man,' I warned. 'He's a bastard with a reputation.'

'You will approach your friend normally, Mr Paris. We are adequate to any unpleasantness.'

I walked up the path that ran across the grass. It was littered with crushed cans and the wrappings of take-away meals. The rain was splashing up off the concrete. Willy, Nelson and Frank were following me, Frank still carrying the toolbox. We climbed the staircase and I addressed the entry phone. Charlie's voice was fuzzed but recognisable, like a man wearing a false beard. He opened the door and stared straight past me at my three companions.

'Don't worry,' I said. 'It's all right. It's all under control.'

'You shouldn't have done this, Angelo. You really shouldn't.'

'Is he inside?'

Charlie nodded. I put my arm round his shoulder and drew him out into the corridor. Then I gestured Willy and the boys into the flat, indicating the room down the hall where guests were customarily entertained.

'You will wait here.' Willy's voice ran very low, like a river far off. 'I shall alert you shortly.'

They went in and shut the door after them. Charlie and I were left outside. I offered him a cigarette, which he took.

I leant on the banisters above the stairwell; metal railings, and below them a pit winding downwards. 'It had to be done,' I told him. 'Things were getting out of control. Mick tried to kill me this morning.'

'No he didn't,' said Charlie.

'He got someone to deliver a bomb to me. It went off.'

'No he didn't,' Charlie repeated. Then he asked vaguely – 'Where do you think I've been getting my money from since Nicola left?'

'That's your affair. Just don't give me any of it.'

'We tried to blackmail someone,' he giggled. 'It worked.'

'Who?'

'The man who bought the body. It was too good an opportunity to pass up.'

'How?'

Charlie was leaning beside me on the banisters. He talked with a sort of hypnotised weariness, as though he'd been waiting up in a hospital for days and nights and had finally received the news of the close of a lingering life. 'I took the registration number of his car. Mick knows a bent copper who'll run a trace for a tenner. He traced it to a woman called Edwina Letherbridge and told Mick where she lived. He went along there the next Saturday afternoon and saw Letherbridge himself mowing the lawn. Hopped over the fence and demanded a thousand pounds.

'It was strange. He gave it to us. He seemed positively glad to be relieved of his money.'

'And where do I fit in?'

'He – Letherbridge – turned funny on us. He started talking nonsense – saying that he was invulnerable, that he wasn't being hurt enough. He said there was no point in his paying us any more because we couldn't damage him. He offered us cash, though, for your address. He said he wanted to contact you.'

'He's heard of me then?' I felt both flattered and uneasy – the paradoxical thrill of having drawn the attention of those on high.

'He's heard of everyone.'

'Who is he?' I asked. It was like asking for a description of a mythical beast.

'I don't know anything about him. I don't know why he bought the body. I don't even know if he was responsible for the murder. He just meant a good source of income to me. But that's finished now. Well and truly fucked.' He tapped a flaccid curl of ash off his cigarette. We watched it spiral down the stairwell, disintegrating as it went. 'What are they doing to Mick?'

'Torturing him, I expect.'

'What for?'

'For what you've just told me. Pointless, isn't it?'

'Are you going to tell them to stop?'

'No,' I said. 'They're enjoying themselves.'

Willy and Frank carried Mick out. He hung vertically between them, his feet dragging. His bearers both clutched an inert arm across their shoulders. They struggled sideways through the door, a comical crucifixion tableau. Nelson wavered ineffectually in attendance. Willy was panting a little and sorely vexed by his burden of stubborn flesh.

'Thirty-seven steps,' I remarked helpfully.

'Not true, actually,' Charlie corrected. 'Mick counted them wrong. He was a couple out.'

'I was not born to manual labour,' said Willy. 'Mr Paris, would you be so kind? You recall that Simon of Cyrene – who is reputed to have been black – helped on a similar occasion. I am requesting you to repay this debt.'

'Is he dead?' I asked.

'No. He is merely a little unconscious. It is traditional to break a malefactor's legs. This we did, partly to ensure that he does not trouble you in the foreseeable future.'

'I'll bet he's a vicious bugger with a crutch.'

'It may be so, Mr Paris. Now, would you please?'

I cautiously replaced Willy, my left arm round Mick's waist and my right clamping his wrist to my shoulder. Farewells were bade to Charlie and we shuffled down the staircase. I wondered whether Willy's discomfiture had been caused by the weight or by the very discernible stink of sweat-sodden, piss-permeated clothing.

'Let's dump the fucker,' I suggested halfway down.

'We must persevere to the end. We shall deposit him discreetly. However, as a concession to your nostrils, he will travel in the boot.'

A task we eventually achieved. Under the dull glow of a streetlight, the unceased rain wriggling its fingers under my collar, we folded Mick up like a collapsible stool and stowed him away. And we drove back to Eth's, Willy telling me what I already knew as we went.

I was thinking about this man – the stone man – the Stone Age man; this banal, bullying admixture of cowardice and brutality who had tried to kill me but who had acquiesced so easily to blackmail. Who had visited Nina and then delivered a thunderbolt that had missed me by a fraction.

102

Whose monumental bulk lumbered through this tale, putting events in process, like a giant rolling rocks down a hillside whilst we poor mortals scurried in the valley below. I tried to apprehend his mind, but could only visualise it as some primitive machine – a water-wheel or a mill – something turning or grinding, rotating massively. He was a merciless, unimaginative demi-god to whom the clubs and flints of his ancestors had grunted with simple, articulate barbarity. A man who used crude implements to survive.

My speculations snapped. A girl ran across the road in front of the car; damp brakes' squeaking and the tyres slithering. She was only a hundred yards from Eth's flat but already her blouse was drenched and adhering to her narrow body – nipples grey and chilled into prominence under the thin fabric. Willy leaned over and threw open the passenger door.

'Go back to your young lady,' he ordered. 'I must retrieve my property.'

I charged down the street with a glorious, bullish indelicacy; charged to Eth's flat, where all the doors were flung open. Eth was standing motionless in the lounge, a press cutting held in her left hand.

'She's left you!' I cried triumphantly. 'She's left you and Willy's got her back!'

'I only showed her this,' said Eth, speaking with an introspective hushedness, as if attempting to explain to herself a devastating, incomprehensible disaster. She seemed for a moment utterly desolate, like someone on a lonely highway beside a wrecked car. 'So she would be sure I had friends. Friends who could protect us both.'

She didn't stir when I took it from her. It was a clipping from a local newspaper – a photograph of her smiling and shaking hands with a statue. Or what looked like a statue. And below it was the caption – 'Ethel Spurgeon welcomes Detective Inspector Donald Letherbridge of the Anti-Terrorist Squad to the Battersea Women's Centre.'

Part Two

12

'Why,' I asked, 'was she so frightened by this?' I flapped the photograph gently, a gull's wing undulation on the dense night air.

'Because. . .' Eth muttered, 'because . . .' She stood with her head down and her hands unclutched at her sides, in the classic posture of despair. 'Consorting with the enemy.'

'A min?' I ventured carelessly.

'Fuck off. Worse than that.'

'A minotaur?' A mythological caricature undoubtedly dear to her. And certainly it was possible to believe that, below the policeman's trunk, there was a blue-clad bull's body equipped with two pairs of boots.

'Closer,' she said. 'Don't you recognise him?'

'Nope,' I told her. 'Can't say I do.'

'And you've had him described to you twice,' she said. 'And you still don't know who it is.'

'Nope.' Not even trying to puzzle it out. I was gratified, in fact, by my own ignorance. It seemed to sever all responsibility from me.

'The man who beat her up. The man, therefore, by extension, who bought the body off Charlie. Who's a member of the Anti-Terrorist Squad and so, probably, at some remove, the perpetrator of your bomb. And' – she pointed distressfully at the picture – a rain-lashed gesture, struck through a storm – 'that's me. That's me shaking hands with him.'

107

Here at last, then, in this curiously dead, autumnal newspaper clipping, I had my first visible trace of the legendary Stone Man. My would-be assassin. I had expected something monstrous – a Yeti, at least. But the fact of the matter was that he looked – there was no other word for it – human. His hair was white like a splash of milk on his brow. He had eyes to which I instantly attributed greyness and a smile showing the sort of honest teeth that seemed destined to bite into apples. He could have been, and probably was, an uncle. Somebody's, anyway.

'You see,' persisted Eth, 'how damaging you've been? Your drunken jests – Eth the Death and all that? They made sense enough to her when she saw the picture. Me and her attacker shaking hands.'

Between happenstance and me Eth had been caught, as if she had strayed across a projector's beam and found herself tainted by its light. She had lost Nina in part, admittedly, because of my mischievousness; but also because from the start she had been more deeply involved than she knew. She was discovering with horror her own footprints on a path in the forest where she had no recollection of ever having been.

Poor Eth, so pure – it was a calamity for her. I had a premonition she would construe this accident as a moral verdict.

'It connects,' she announced. And collapsed into an armchair felled by a spectral swipe.

It was not a room furnished to witness defeat. The suite – three piece – was covered in leather. Broad red and black stripes. Triffidic plants sprayed out their spiked and solid leaves, and pinned blatantly to the wall was a poster of two Soviet women workers dragging a horse, head turned aside, towards socialism. It was a room that seemed positively to broach the future.

'Look,' I comforted her. 'Coincidence.' Although our relations were antagonistic, I didn't want to win. I relished the struggle too much. I was trying to offer her the strength to carry on. I hated to see her this dispirited. 'I was pissed and I said something silly. Nina's drug-shredded brain . . . You know how it is.'

'There's no such thing as coincidence. Letherbridge, Nina, the Centre – they all touch me. They all connect in me. Go and make some coffee.'

'It's been a long day. Full of explosions.'

'Think,' she insisted. 'We must think.'

I succumbed and slouched with a loud and patient sigh to the kitchen, leaving her, one elbow propped on the arm of her chair, her cheek on the palm of her hand. I suspected that she longed quietly to burst into tears – to mourn, perhaps, the passing of another belief. I filled the kettle.

She had believed – what? That goodwill alone would suffice? That a blind and muscular integrity would bring the corrupt edifice down? That, somehow, the world would prove to be as honest as she was? As free of those ironies that returned like a dog, snapping at the ankles?

It hardly mattered now. I plugged the kettle in and recollected how many times belief – that Puritanical device – had sabotaged our dealings. Once, in a narrow, temporary room when I had goosestepped up and down – holding a black comb between nose and upper lip – reciting the opening lines of Hitler's long-lost novel:

'Nigger the Jew ate her child slowly. It vozz her last dietorial claim of the evening . . .'

'You think you're being funny, I suppose?' A frequent question of Eth's, to which the answer was usually, 'Yes.'

She walked out on me. Marched out, in fact, with the startling and storming swiftness of an army on night-time manoeuvres. A week later I received a letter – so sermonic and pompous it could have been composed by her ecclesiastical father – ending, 'Contact me again when you are less of a racist or when fewer of my friends are Jewish.'

I replied on a sheet of writing paper which I had embellished – top right-hand corner – with a negress's head. And, underneath, the legend 'Actors Against Wogs and Women'. Tease tease tease. Push to the limits. And no communication for a year.

The kettle wheezed to orgasm like an old man. I unplugged it and poured the water, lively and bubbular, into a pair of mugs – finding in this something crudely appropriate. Then I returned to the lounge where Eth – I swear it – was harshly swallowing salt, mucosal tears.

'Don't blame yourself,' I advised her.

'You,' she said. 'You.' And, abbreviated though the accusation was, I understood it fully.

Then she laughed. An unusual, bitter event. A laugh to the ceiling, eyes looking upward through their tear-spangled geometry as if accepting a riddled challenge inscribed there. Her shoulders flicked and dropped; a gesture to shrug off a cloak.

I placed a cup of coffee on the small table beside her, clunking it down with the deliberation of an initiatory pawn's move. 'Did you know,' I began, 'that Charlie and Mick were blackmailing him?'

It was my way of hinting that this affair, with its own crippled motion, rambled around beyond her; that there were more faults in the world than hers.

'He invited himself,' she said. 'He rang up and said "Me and the lads would like to do something for you." I thought for a moment it was an indecent proposition; then I accepted. Why did I accept?'

'He must be a remarkable man.'

'He explained to me about the money. About the role of the police in the community. He enthused about the cause. And he stressed it had to be at short notice.'

'God,' I commented. 'So much bullshit. Pigshit, rather. What was he like?'

I felt sure, even at this distance, like Marlowe winding down the river towards Kurtz, that the key to the mystery lay in his resonant psychology. I had made an idol of him – fashioned him in my imagination as a shape magnificent and shadowed. I was convinced, moreover, that we merely

110

had to approach him, tap his hollow chest, and it would emit a boom. A boom like my bomb – inarticulate and unmistakable – wherein all kinds of secrets could be read.

'Very restrained. He was the only one who didn't drink at lunch. He sat there throughout the meal as if he was clenching his arse.

'All the rest of them were drunk or getting that way. They started telling jokes – like "What do black youths and arthritis have in common?" It made me sick. Sick that we had to accept charity from these men.'

'What do they have in common?' I enquired. 'It could be important.'

'Fortunately, we had a co-opted member of the local council's committee on racist humour with us. She explained that these things aren't funny any more.'

'Then what?'

'They started singing "These boots are made for walking". It was very threatening.'

I smirked, seeing it differently from her. They sounded like Joe Dante's gremlins, voices hoarse and provocative, doing exactly what they knew was wickedest. Endearing little monsters. And the women, shocked to their conscientious souls, wondering how to rid themselves of this irrepressible infestation.

'He stopped them. He simply said, "That's not what we came for." He said it very quietly, almost in a whisper, but the message got through. One by one, they shut up. The last of them got to the line "walk all over you"; then he put his hand up to his mouth, paled, and looked very chastened. They stayed quiet even when he left us.'

'Left you?'

'Letherbridge. He went for a walk. He claimed the smoke was making him dizzy.'

'Didn't that strike you as odd?'

'He was a strange man.'

'Yes,' I concurred. 'A strange man.'

I was in that uncomfortable state of being neither drunk

111

nor sober. A no man's land, where inebriation's check-point police have stamped your papers and expelled you in disgrace, whilst sobriety's dour bureaucrats still eye you uneasily from another border. And the day's events, on whisky-coloured horses, carouselled in slow deceleration round my skull. I wanted to piss a lot, also, which was distracting me. Nevertheless, I could perceive that something – more than one thing – was amiss.

'You accept,' I proposed, certain of my footing, 'that these men hated you?'

'Yes. Of course.'

'And yet. Letherbridge – this stern old sod – dragged them out one morning to pedal bikes for you. It doesn't fit.'

I had seen an inconsistency – a curiosity – like the shimmer of a fish's scales in a khaki pond. I wanted to put my hand on it – to produce it palpably for Eth. It was a matter of finding the right verbal formulation. 'Look,' I said. And stopped.

'What?'

'Dammit. He's a respectable man. If he does anything for charity he does it for the respectable ones. Poppies, donkeys in distress, things like that. But not wimmin. Wimmin, unlike donkeys, are political.'

'I explained the politics of it. Publicity. Christ, give me credit for understanding publicity.'

'Secrecy,' I suggested. 'That's what you need to under-stand. The things that happen under the robes of politics and righteousness. It's always a good idea to peep under the robes. See what the hands are up to.'

'What were they up to, then?'

'I don't know. I'll tell you this, though: it wasn't charity. Letherbridge wanted to speak to someone or to find something at your refuge. And that's why he offered himself at such short notice,' – it was all coming in a rush now – 'because the need arose after the murder. And one more thing – he didn't leave the table because of the smoke.'

112

'How do you know?'

'Nina and Charlie both told us he smoked cigars; and Nina had the burns to prove it. A man who smokes cigars doesn't get to feel dizzy because of a little cigarette smoke.'

Dawn subsided into the sky like a sad sponge cake, brown-orange and saturated, collapsing into its filling. And, by then, I had decided that it was proper for Eth to go to work and find out.

'Find out what?' she demanded pertinently.

'Well, we can assyoome' – the assumption switchbacked over a suppressed yawn – 'three things: that Letherbridge went to your centre, place, whatever, for a reason connected with the murder; that, during his absence from the table, he threatened someone or removed something or otherwise procured a silence. Do you keep files?'

'Of course we do. We're a professional organisation.'

'Then find out which one's missing. Talk to whoever it was that handled the case. Because – and this is our third assumption, the only one that makes sense of the first two – my guess is that the girl who was killed was once at your hostel, thingy, home. And, consequently, Letherbridge offered to come and do the charity bit so as he would have an opportunity to snaffle any record there was of her.'

'And whilst I'm looking for something that isn't there, what will you be doing?'

'My dear girl – sleeping.' To emphasise the point I kicked my shoes off. I felt my feet expanding – I could almost believe I heard them sigh. I began to unpick a sock from between my clammy toes.

Eth had once declared, 'Angelo, your feet smell' – thereby giving a hostage to fortune. For, although there can be no excuse for a physical feature so blatantly irredeemable, I had found a way of turning it to my advantage. Whenever I wanted to get rid of her I simply intimated that I was about to take my socks off. It usually assured her flight. This time, however, it failed.

'You're coming with me.' That custodial voice again.

'Sleep!' I protested. 'That knits up the baffled sleeve of care. You can't take me to that sanctuary of wimmin. I'm a min, don't forget. I'll walk around exposing myself, I promise.'

'I'll buy you some crayons and a colouring-in book and lock you in my office. I want you there.'

'Wh-i-i-y?' I pleaded, in my best brat's whine.

'I'm not having you sleeping while I'm hard at work. That's that.'

'All right,' I conceded. I became suddenly serious. 'On one condition. Tell me what black youths and arthritis have in common.'

Eth half turned away. She was embarrassed, like a little girl asked to repeat what the filthy old tramp had just said to her. She mumbled quickly – 'They both attack old ladies.'

The bus, like a bronchial lung, coughed us to Battersea. We sat on the upper deck; people like soft tumours jogged by the hacking rhythm. Behind my left ear I could hear a set of gums engaged in toothless, ceaseless, champing mastication. I had a bottle of Scotch – a quarter full and surreptitiously purloined – hidden inside my coat, and I was afraid the bus's jolts would cast it up before Eth's censorious eyes. It was a tense journey.

It transpired, as we travelled, that my abduction was not wholly punitive. Eth had plans to put me to work constructively. I was to search through the file index, checking that there was a report corresponding to each entry, whilst she talked to what she called 'our long-term residents'.

'The real fucking cripples,' I commented sourly.

'Damn you, Angelo. Have you forgotten why we're doing this?'

'Yes.'

'Justice.' The word rang resolutely along the upper deck, like a sword clashed on a shield. 'Justice for Karen and for women like her.'

114

'We British,' I informed her, 'have never believed in justice. We believe in the law. We're a very concrete nation.'

I rested my head against the throbbing window and thought how true this was. Justice – one of those big words which make us so unhappy. A continental notion to boot, and probably unavailable on this island. And Eth was foredoomed, in her pursuit of a metaphysic, to failure. She was chasing something you can neither see, nor feel, nor taste.

I, however, had begun to understand my own involvement. It had come to me as an insidious revelation in the early, early morning. And it was, quite simply, that I wanted to solve the puzzle. I didn't feel myself harassed by danger – although Letherbridge, presumably, had tried to kill me. In fact, his bomb struck me as strangely flippant – laughable, even. A joke between friends. I was dispassionately intrigued, as if beckoned by a ghost to a walled-up door. I felt like a visitor in a castle, summoned to aid in the disinterment of a concealed, forgotten past.

We got off the bus and walked across the lawn, and into that low, flat building, where sounds seemed to soak into the walls, the ceilings, like ink into blotting paper. Eth's hand hovered constantly near my left elbow, as if I were a defector being chaperoned through uncertain borderlands. The bottle of Scotch bulged, suspicious as a gun beneath my coat. All the clichés of a spy movie. I could almost imagine that the silence was caused by some fern-fronded, pine-needled forest floor – a greenery so dense it inhaled noises.

Eth shoved me into her office. 'We'll have this sorted out in an hour or two,' she declared. And I realised why it was that I was tired and she wasn't.

She had scented an ending. She seemed to imagine that a solution, as apprehensible and as prepared as a dinner, was waiting for us up the road. So she was keen to hurry, to go

115

without sleep, for this short, final distance. But I was weary and had to be dragged because I suspected that at the end we would find only that we had finished; the puzzle over and everything left in place.

I had sat down behind Eth's desk, feeling that unoccupied unease of someone who has arrived at a new job and hasn't yet been told what to do.

'Take your coat off,' she suggested.

'No thanks. It's too cold in here.'

'Have some of that Scotch you're hiding. It should warm you up.'

She clattered four box files down in front of me. 'This is our index. One sheet per person. It gives her name, the names of the social workers involved, and the name of the half-way house worker, where appropriate. The detailed reports are in that cabinet there.'

'What the fuck's a half-way house worker?'

'It's someone – usually not a professional social worker – who helps victims of violence integrate back into the community.'

'Ah yes. Integrate. Community. I'll bear it in mind.'

'And one other thing: you are not – repeat, not – to read any of the reports. Just find out which one's missing. I'm going to go and talk to some people.' She announced it as though talking to people were something which, like climbing a mountain, you set about with ice picks and rope.

I lit a cigarette, poured myself a drink and considered the methodology of this tiresome task. It was best accomplished, I concluded, on the floor. I extracted an entire drawer (A–D) from Eth's cabinet, chucked a file down beside it and commenced – ignoring, of course, that ban as tempting as a fairytale prohibition.

I began with Antonia Abellanos – an Argentinian exile. During the Falklands War her husband had forbidden her to approach within a hundred feet of the marital bed. Obediently the poor woman had confined herself to a tent at the bottom of the garden but – one night as she slept – her husband had bombarded her with fresh tomatoes on the grounds that she constituted a threat to his sexual security. A sad little story with a sadder postscript in an unknown hand: 'Husband believes himself to be a submarine. Differences irreconcilable.'

Anecdotes of violence accumulated on the carpet. White pages fanned out like dovetails; vignettes of brutality played out in cramped conditions; small insanities breeding like mice in the tenements. Here a man who was convinced his lover had poisoned their child. Here another who, just because he was drunk, believed he would never find a job. So many reasons attributed to the sudden swinging of an arm or the arc of a foot. It seemed that society – like the weather, ubiquitous, indifferent and unable to be charged in court – was responsible for much.

Crosslegged amidst these intractable problems, I found nothing missing. Two hours had gone by and I was on the Es. The whisky was nearly drained and I had one cigarette left. Drifting, drifting; bumping downstream on sleep's recurrent sandbanks. I decided to get a breath of fresh air.

I went down the corridor and along to the window where, once before, I had seen those two women, perpetual knitters, sitting. They were still there, their slow scarves racing like slugs across the floor. I stood and watched them – the rapid bitter clicking of their needles – until one of them, without looking up, raised a yellow hand to beckon me.

I went into some sort of common room – spacious and deliberately informal. The two women at the far end were drawn up level to each other on blue leatherette chairs. I walked over to them.

One of them – dressed in a purple crimplene suit – nodded to her shopping bag. It was filled with balls of wool.

'You've got young hands,' she said. 'You untangle it for me. She tangles it up when I'm asleep. To hinder me during the day.'

'I do not.' The other, indignant. 'I don't need to.'

Their heads, on flesh-flapped, scrawny necks, seemed to duck and peck at each other. I pulled a ball of wool out of the first one's bag and began picking at its knots.

'Don't you go helping her,' said the other. 'That's not fair. She doesn't need any help.'

Silently I let the wool fall. 'What are your names, ladies?' I asked.

'I'm called Edna,' answered the first. 'And she's called Edna too. So I'm called Eddie to avoid confusion.'

'Good.' I'd seen detectives on TV dealing with batty old ladies; their methodical, doubly clear politeness. 'I wonder if you could try and remember something for me. A girl who used to be here, before Miss Spurgeon came, called Karen.' I issued the official description – the one given to Eth by Nicola, repeated by Eth so faithfully in the Pacific.

Eddie and Edna began to laugh. It was a complacent, broken cackle. 'That sort of description's no use to us,' they told me. 'We're both blind. We gave up seeing long ago.'

I looked at their eyes and saw that it was true. Plastic, joke-shop eyes, focused neither on knitting nor on me; and black, pin-head pupils, each threaded to a different line.

'Tell us what she was really like. How she spoke. How her footsteps sounded.'

And I realised how powerless I was genuinely to describe her. In spite of my – what? – interest. Obsession. I had seen her only in death, besmirched by blood; seen her in fantasy and heard her talked about. But I hadn't got to the heart of the matter. I seemed still to be dealing with the image – reflected, insubstantial – and not the thing itself.

'She spoke nicely. I imagine her walk was brisk.'

'I must have touched her face. I always touch their faces. The young girls.' Eddie. Her left hand stretched out in the air, tracing the eyelids, the nose, the lips of our invisible Karen. Her breath started coming faster, reminding me of a bird's wing beating against a window. 'In the face you can feel the lostness, the going from here to there. All the

118

young girl's faces float, you see. Yes.' She subsided back in her chair.

'Do you have a name for me?' I asked, lapsing into this mediumistic dialect.

'Yes,' she said. 'I've remembered her now. Her name was Karen Jones.'

'Jones!' I was incredulous at my own gullibility. 'Fucking typical. The commonest, the safest. Is there anyone here who knew a Jones?' I got up angrily to leave, with the bitterness of having thrown my money away in a gypsy's tent.

'Ah, but my dear,' said Edna, 'that wasn't her real name. We've only given you her false one.'

When Eth returned to her office I was dozing on the floor, a single sheet held in a deadened hand. The bang of the door, the scattered papers rising, rustling, woke me. I held the sheet out to her.

'The weird sisters spoke true.'

'Angelo, Angelo, you're babbling again.' From those words alone I knew she hadn't been successful.

'Not so. Jones, Karen – no corresponding file. It has to be the girl. The most banal pseudonym imaginable.'

'And who was the social worker involved?'

'Stuff the social worker. We ought to talk to the half-assed house worker. Who led her with pastoral hand back to this world of sin.'

'Who was that?'

'One Frances Dugdale.'

'Frances Dugdale,' Eth repeated enigmatically. She seemed glad to have a secret of her own to clasp. 'But she's one of our best . . . our most active . . .' Her voice trailed towards a meaningless pause. Then she added, as though this were the most curious thing of all, 'I've even met her.'

13

We had been following, from the start, things that weren't there: a vanished body, the page gone from the Bible in her room (along with those other careful obliterations of her identity), a missing diary, a stolen file. Our most tangible clues were absences – hollows carved in the air where the object itself had been put a moment before. It was as if we were gasping uphill on a treasure hunt, discovering at every stage that the hint we needed had just been snatched away and that, therefore, all we could do was stagger on in the direction where we thought the next riddle might lie. And this, I pointed out to Eth, in pursuit of a man who couldn't possibly have committed the murder – because he too wasn't there. He hadn't been, could not have been, at the party.

'But he's behind it,' she insisted.

And I thought immediately of a screen. Shadows, grey-edged and porous, the shapes of hands and fingers, playing across it. And what we had to do had become an act of vandalism. Blasting through the screen's taut skin to surprise the puppeteer behind it.

It was the day after our latest, greatest discovery. The evening, in fact. We were going up the staircase to Frances Dugdale's flat and I was reflecting how strange it was that everyone seemed to live in flats nowadays – and upper-storey ones at that. Transitory, haphazard existences, I supposed. Nothing nailed down. A multitude of interchangeable shelves, shuffling themselves across the city so that it was impossible to locate or to name a fixed life, to be sure that it would still be there tomorrow.

Eth knocked on the door – dark blue, wooden, four panes of reinforced glass set in it. The door opened on a short chain. A woman stared at us with aggressive timidity – her hair close-cropped, spiky, abruptly short and her features flat and pale; a basic face, as if drawn by a lazy hand. She was wearing square-cut dungarees that gave her a box-like, robotic appearance. She reminded me of a convict or a Maoist peasant – someone who had decided it would be prudent not to think too much.

'I suppose you've come about the girl,' she said. Her tone was such that we might as well have been answering a small advertisement in a For Sale column. Neither of us replied to her.

Frances looked at us with a cornered sullenness. She was contemplating perhaps, the arrival of a tardy but inevitable retribution – something like the reappearance of an old debt, eluded for so long but never shaken off.

'Come in,' she eventually conceded, and took the chain down.

We followed her down the hallway, past the bathroom, whence we could hear the sizzling sounds of someone washing her – his? – hair, and into the lounge, where a cyclopean television stared at us gigantically. A rectangle of carpet stretched its frayed threads towards the walls. The sofa, springs thrusting up through its fabric like worm casts, was of the kind that invites you to sit on the floor.

I slouched against the wall by the door, hands in pockets, thinking it might be fun to look dangerous. I wished I'd bought that hat I'd once promised myself. Eth sat neatly on a hard-backed chair. Her black briefcase – so bureaucratically threatening, so possibly full of damning documents – laid across her knees.

Frances was standing in the middle of the room, rolling a cigarette between blunt fingers. No tobacco spilling. She did it with such concentrated parsimony that she seemed to be forewarning us that we would get nothing for free.

'What do you know about her?' asked Eth. 'Where did she come from? The file was stolen.'

'Go and talk to the social workers. They'll tell you.'

'We're asking you,' I said, trying to snarl.

'There were plenty who passed through your hands before her.' Eth extracted a sheaf of papers tidied together like a guillotine's blade from her briefcase. 'When did it become a commercial enterprise? When did you start selling them to Willy?'

'Find out for yourselves.'

Then silence. It was difficult to believe we had played our cards so quickly. I had expected, at least, a confrontation. And here we were, each having said a line or two, confounded by the fact that we had reached a limit.

And yet, there was something puzzling about Frances's manner. She had blocked us absolutely; we couldn't compel her to talk. But she seemed, curiously, to have a sense of an impending revelation. She looked as if she was awaiting a blow which neither Eth nor I could see how to deliver.

'You know who we're talking about,' I ventured, 'although we haven't mentioned her name. And you haven't asked who I am. I know you've met Eth before, but shouldn't you have been surprised to see us? For the sake of form, anyway?'

Frances, shielding her cigarette in a cupped hand, considered me with ironic resentment, as if she had always anticipated I would stumble on this path of reasoning and was merely intrigued to observe how long it would take me to follow it to its end. She had what I could only describe as oppressed shrewdness, smirking at her superior's slowness in spotting her fault.

'Because,' I went on, 'you must have learnt that it was likely we would come some time and you could only have learnt that from someone who was, as it were, on the inside. Someone like Charlie, who had warned Nicola, who is at this moment in your bathroom because' – triumphantly, remembering now with blinding exactitude Charlie's allusions to Nicola's new, dungareed lover – 'you're not Frances at all. You're Fran.'

Fran applauded sardonically. Slow handclaps, her wrists

like sticks between thick denim cuffs. Her cigarette was still between her lips and her eyes were narrowed against its rising smoke. 'So what?' she challenged.

'So it went further back.' Eth had rapidly perceived a configuration of consequences, had grasped them almost as if they were represented visibly, like the foundations of an old building startlingly washed clean of mud. 'Nicola didn't meet the girl by chance. She met her through you. And she'd met you and effectively she'd left Charlie before the party. Those relationships were already in place and what happened that night was merely the culmination of – of something else.' The weakness of her conclusion surprised even herself. She had seen the diagram and it amounted to nothing.

'You and Charlie are still in touch then?' I conjectured. 'There's no rift between him and Nicola? It's still hunky-dory? Still collusion?'

Fran sat down amidst her sofa's arse-ambushing springs, workman-like, her knees apart. All her movements appeared to be calculatedly abrasive, as if she had sand-papered them once upon a time; a body whose every motion gestured 'Fuck you, brother'.

The door beside me opened and Nicola halted there, turbaned in a yellow towel. Her pink face steamed into deeper pinkness. She was short, plump and blonde, so that when she had been with Charlie she had always reminded me obliquely of a golden beach ball. She was wearing, now, a turquoise silk dressing gown embroidered with a single scarlet dragon. And beneath it she seemed to have acquired a certain physical hardness.

'Hi,' I said.

She stayed trapped in the doorway, like someone hesitating before fording a stream. It was the same unease as Fran had first exhibited. She was waiting, I guessed, for a sign from Fran – who had, in a sense, already crossed over – an indication that it was safe to step in. She gave Fran an under-the-eyebrows glance that asked – I suspected – 'Have they found out yet?'

'Come in,' Fran reassured her. 'Join us.'

'You lied to me,' Eth accused – an accusation at least as recriminatory as it was investigative, made to a friend who had merited it through treachery. 'It was no accident that Karen was at that party.'

Nicola went and sat down next to Fran on the hazardous sofa. Fran touched her on the arm. A touch halfway between that of a sharp lawyer and a possessive protectress. 'You don't have to tell them anything,' she said.

'Fuck you, Fran baby!' I stormed. I was suddenly jealous – not for myself, but for Charlie. I was seized with a premonition that Charlie would sink – indeed, had already started sinking – as a consequence of Nicola's having left him. I had a strange, powerful vision of him scrabbling on a cliff face. Blackmail money; sliding, sliding.

'It began by chance,' said Nicola. 'That bit was true.' She had decided to speak but, although I could hear the words, it was to Eth they were really addressed. A last tribute to an old bond, settled as a private transaction. Even Fran was marginal to this. Nicola was talking as if recalling the actions of someone she distantly remembered once having been.

'I met Fran by chance in just the way I told you I'd met Karen. That was why the lie was so easy to tell – I simply swapped the names around. And it all happened earlier – not the Thursday before the party – another Thursday a month or so before that. The rest's true though – what's left of it.'

She paused for a moment to contemplate that vanishing residue. It must have been like tracing out a shadow as it dissolved beneath a disappearing sun. 'If it had been a different bar. If Angelo had been in when I called. None of this.' She shook her head. 'None of this.'

Fran, it transpired, had wanted Nicola to go home with her that evening. It sounded, to me, a savage, graceless seduction – as if there had been a declaration of physical intent between them which neither had bothered to

124

embroider; undoubtedly straight and to the point, except that there had been an obstacle.

And that was how Karen was first referred to in the story – 'an obstacle'. The terminology wasn't lost on Eth. I glanced at her and saw that it had registered acutely. She had clawed the phrase towards her like a gambling chip and I was sure that she would shortly cash it in.

For myself, though, I was remembering Nicola's frequent, disastrous schemes; how she had reputedly sold quarter grammes of talcum powder to German hippies on the Ponte Vecchio; how once, when working in a pub, she had invented a regular and given him a slate behind the bar; how she had conjured out of her imagination an East African republic – called, I believe, Melanka – and collected outside the LSE on behalf of its political prisoners. I hadn't forgotten, either, her absurd dating agency. It struck me that, in an off-beat sort of way, Karen may have been its only client.

'The obstacle', anyway, was staying at Fran's. And it was here that I began to understand why Nicola had chosen her particularly distanced mode of narration, as if she were on top of a hill describing the activities of a village far below. She was – it couldn't be avoided – guilty. She was referring to a Nicola who had conspired with Fran to get rid of the obstacle.

'To get rid of her!' Eth exclaimed, misunderstanding dramatically.

'No,' Nicola told her. 'We weren't murderers.'

It was more sordidly convenient than that. Nicola was heavily in debt; she had lost her bar job (another spectral customer? I wondered) and those letters from the bank were arriving at the rate of two a week and operating with the perpetual, dangerous suction of a downstream current.

(I remembered receiving a sequence of them once myself – ignoring them all – and still they came. Eventually I had been compelled to write to my bank manager to point out that I was taking no cognisance of his threats. I imagined

125

that now, somewhere, my overdraft lay neglected like a disused cellar, growing grey and fungal. But I remembered, too, how desperate I'd been under the first torrent of creditor's letters. I'd considered getting a proper job.)

Nicola, however, had found another solution – one intertwined perversely, lovingly with the problem. The problem, she assured us, was Charlie. She spoke of his 'financial exactions' as if he were a wicked feudal lord – an irresistible force for consumption. His nose dominated the landscape. It rose like a castle, greedier day by day, and it snuffled up the harvest. I could see that she was haunted by Charlie's nose. She glanced twice towards the door as if she feared it might, at any moment, wriggle into our midst and vacuum up the contents of the room. To satiate the nose she went regularly to Brixton.

'I got to know this dealer,' she continued. 'He was always pressurising me. Telling me how he could arrange for me to get the stuff free. In return for . . . in exchange for . . .'

'Sex,' Fran concluded brutally. 'Fucking. No one's immune.'

'So I thought of Karen. I thought I could hand her over to them. Get rid of her and earn myself some money. In one go.'

'Give the girl a career,' I suggested sweetly.

'The dealer introduced me to this pimp. He explained it all to me. He was very pleasant. He's got two daughters himself. He explained – '

But I didn't need to hear how Willy had convinced her. He was, after all, amongst other things, a used-car salesman. I could see him spreading his hands reasonably, as if they represented a natural process like the unfolding of a leaf. I could hear him saying to Nicola (as she faithfully repeated it):

'There is nothing dishonourable in prostitution. After all, in any form of physical employment, what do we do? We sell the use of our bodies for a period of time. A bricklayer sells his hands, his legs, his back – even a little portion of his brain. A prostitute sells – how shall I put it? – the more intimate sections of her body. But she is well rewarded for this invasion of her privacy and, unlike in the building trade, the work is not seasonal.'

'He offered me cash for the introduction,' Nicola continued. ' "The introduction", he called it. He explained how he would find a flat for her, how he would pay her. He never specified what she would have to do.'

'You knew, though,' Eth insisted. 'You're not pretending that you didn't know? Sex? Fucking? From which no one's immune.' She seemed to be inflicting the words like lacerations on herself.

'She knew,' Fran affirmed in a tone of voice as of an adult refusing – absolutely refusing – to let a child escape on the plea of moral imbecility.

'It was your conspiracy too, Fran baby,' I reminded her.

'We led her away,' said Nicola. 'She didn't say anything. She just came along with us. All the time – on the bus – Fran and I – we were saying to ourselves that it was in her best interests really. The right thing to do. And she just sat there, almost as if she could tell. And we left her with the pimp. We didn't wait to see what happened to her.'

I noticed that she had used exactly the language in which anguished owners describe how they've put down a dog.

'And not forgetting,' I conjectured, 'the cash. On delivery.'

'No,' said Nicola. 'Not forgetting that.'

She removed her yellow turban. Her thick, blonde curls settled wetly down around her circular face. Oddly enough, rather than revealing herself, as it were, naturally to us, she looked as though she had mysteriously assumed a wig.

'I think you've told them quite enough,' said Fran.

I waited for Eth to speak. I felt, somehow, that it was her right – that she had a prior claim on this conversation. But she didn't say anything. She sat stiff on her stiff-backed

127

chair, briefcase across her knees and hands folded over it, unable to pronounce a verdict. Perhaps at last she had perceived a moral complication. I spoke up instead –

'You've told us the middle,' I informed them. 'But what about the beginning? And the end?'

'What do you mean?' asked Nicola, who seemed penitently eager to please.

'Eth said,' I reminded her, 'that it was no accident that Karen was at the party. You haven't responded to that at all. And you haven't told us where the girl came from or what she was running from. You've given us a touching little tale – I admit that. But it's only the glue. Where are the two things it connects?'

'She's told you enough.'

'Will you shut the fuck up for a minute, Fran baby? I'm talking to Nicola.'

'Are you going to have us tortured then? Like you got Willy and the boys to torture poor old Mick.'

'Yes. You particularly, Fran baby. We'll pull your pubic hairs out one by one.' And, just to let her know that it hadn't passed me by, I added, 'So Charlie told you that too? You're on pretty good terms with him considering you stole his woman.'

'Piss off. Get out of my house. We're not telling you anything more.'

'Doesn't Nicola have a say in this?' I appealed.

Another silence; then Nicola leaned forward on the sofa, one hand gathering her dressing gown at the throat. Her pink face seemed full of thwarted honesty. The silence was sufficiently long for her to think about speaking, to be on the verge of speaking, to decide not to speak. I measured the three distinct moments before she relapsed back into her seat.

'Come on,' said Eth. 'Let's go.'

'Let me show you to the door,' Nicola offered.

Eth stood up with the weary grimness of a mediator who has heard much, and little to the point, shouted by warring factions. She seemed hugely disappointed, as if by a returned awareness of the capacity human beings evince to squabble over even the largest of issues.

'An obstacle,' she muttered, turning this plastic phrase in her baffled fingers, unsure quite what to do with it. And then, generally, to any of the three of us, 'You should be disgusted with yourself.'

'Bye bye, Fran baby,' I called. 'Next time we'll bring the tweezers.'

I stepped thankfully out of the doorway and down the hall. Eth followed at her more diplomatic pace. And I noticed Nicola slipping in the opposite direction, away from the front door and towards the bedroom at the end of the corridor – a sideways scuttle on her bare feet.

'Wait,' I whispered to Eth.

She halted between two paces. We looked at each other, drawn conspiratorially close by the accident of where she had stopped. I nodded down the hallway, gesturing towards Nicola's disappearance. We were suddenly, sharply aware of how big a threat Fran posed. If she had emerged to find us lingering there – so guiltily close, I reflected, that we could have kissed – we would, for sure, have lost something vital.

Then Nicola hurried on tiptoe back up the hall. Her breath suppressed to timid, shallow gasps. I could almost hear the palpitations of a frightened heart. She was committing, for her, an act of reckless daring.

'Take this,' she said, thrusting a piece of paper at Eth. 'The girl gave it to me just before we sold her. She said it was the secret of her life.'

Eth took it and began bemusedly to fold it.

'And one other thing: the party was for her. It was actually for her. Now go. I've done the best I can.'

And so, with the enticing scent of mysteries crushed small – the very essence of mystery – like perfume on our wrists, we wafted down the staircase to the street below.

'To the pub,' I instructed Eth. 'We have not a moment to lose.'

'It's only nine o'clock,' she protested.

'No matter,' I replied. 'Better late than never.'

I felt buoyant. My feet rebounded off the pavement as though it were made of rubber. A fanfare of cheerfulness was heralding clearly through my bones.

The phenomenon was without precedent in this short history of Angelo Paris. I put it down, decidedly, to the fact that we had at last a palpable clue.

It gave me the feeling that here indeed was something to follow – something that would lead us. It was like discovering the key to playing an amorphous character on the stage. It bestowed a consoling sense of definition – a sense that finally there was a certainty on which we could rely. We had, after all, got hold of nothing less than the secret of a girl's life. It could not be counted as negligible.

I swung through the pub doors. It was one I'd never been in before but had spied, infallibly, as the nearest. It turned out to be a cavernous affair – by an architectural quirk much larger on the inside than it appeared it could possibly be from without; empty now except for a few scattered drinkers who gave the impression that they were stopping off before going somewhere more satisfying – like travellers in a station waiting-room late at night. The furnishings and decorations were predominantly of a muted, mushy green. A little dull gold glimmered on the bar rail and from the polished pump handles, whilst a pair of giant fruit machines trilled to each other soft electronic calls and winked a hundred eyes in garish sequence. I guessed that they were probably in love.

I bought a couple of pints of lager and joined Eth at a circular, wooden table. She was contemplating it as if it were a draughts piece on a problematic board.

'Why did you have to turn it into a confrontation?' she demanded.

'Come on,' I said. 'Confrontation or not, we're getting along fine.'

'No.' (Decisively no.) 'I made up my mind after the last time that we would never get on fine again.'

'But we're friends aren't we?' I bargained.

'No,' she said again. 'We're collaborators.'

'Ah.' I raised my glass to that shabby word – a smear on our relationship, a makeshift compromise between mistrusting parties. 'Cheers. What the hell. Fuck it. Let's look at the clue.'

The clue: which, just a moment ago, had promised to be so exciting. The entrance to a walled and wild garden was now nothing more, perhaps, than a permit to carry on along the road. It had lost its aura. It was only itself; the scrap of paper which Eth unfolded and flattened on the table.

As soon as I saw it I recognised it; I remembered the stump of page I had seen in Karen's Bible, in her room – its zigzags tessellating exactly with the zagzigs of this up-rooted leaf. And, inscribed on it with such Gothic force that one could almost say it was graven, was the following dedication:

'Whatsoever cometh forth of the doors of my house shall surely be the Lord's.'

I stared at it; read it through again, stared at it again. 'This is the secret of her life,' I said. 'It's very good. As a secret.'

It spoke volumes, of course; but only in a massive, shapeless way – like a cloud lumbering across the sky, threatening rain or hail or sleet or snow. It was as though, attached to the girl from the start – wherever that had been, the indefinable start – was this divine pledge, a man's hand clawed in the heavens.

'It means nothing to me,' I confessed.

'But it's almost certainly from the Bible,' Eth declared. 'So there's a chance my father might know what the context is.'

'Why not? Give him a ring.'

I rummaged in my silver-tinkling pocket. Karen was, indirectly anyway, paying for the call. I produced three ten pence pieces and pushed them across the table.

131

Eth went to the public telephones. There were two of them adjacent on the far wall, nailed there like trophies, as if the landlord had personally hunted them down. I watched her walk; her skirt swinging across her calves like a lantern agitated by a recent touch. It was the sort of candid and efficient walk that the private secretaries of great men have. It states, quite categorically, that these legs have dealings with power. Amazing, really, how a decent salary can affect the way someone walks.

She returned unenlightened. 'He says it's probably from the Old Testament and he doesn't know much about that half. There's not much call for it nowadays.'

'Not much call for it!'

'No. It's not considered relevant.'

'Not enough about the evils of unemployment, I suppose.'

Eth folded up our solid clue again. It had proved to be a tantalising fragment, oracular and uninterpretable, like something spoken out of smoke and flame to try the wits of mortals; an obscure synecdoche which Karen had hoped – perhaps had desperately hoped – would impart the whole of the matter.

I felt we had a duty to understand it. Its poignant brevity made me think of a soldier's will. It had been dispatched by the girl before she disappeared, drowned, died; dispensed under the pressure of condensed time. It was as if she had trusted us to understand it, to do her that small justice after her life was ended. And here we were, failing her.

'Do you think,' I said to Eth, 'that she knew she was going to be killed?'

Eth didn't answer me. She was muttering, incanting intensely, 'The party was for her. Actually for her. What's the significance of that?'

'For her benefit? In her honour?' I suggested.

'How does it fit? Why was Charlie holding a party for her? Why was Nicola present? Why's Charlie still speaking to Nicola and Fran?'

'All these questions and many more will be answered in next week's episode of . . .'

'Be serious, Angelo.'

'All right. Let's take it a step at a time.' I drew a long breath. I was about to plunge into deep water. 'There's one thing that binds people more strongly than love or blood or hatred or death or betrayal. It forced Nicola to get rid of the girl like a dog – although she would probably have preferred not to. It got me into this fucking mess. It's called money. If you're looking for connections between disparate people, *cherchez l'argent*.'

I was surprising even myself. It was as if, having trodden shifting sands for so long, I had randomly struck a spade down and had found something harder, more solid and more real than any paper clue – a bedrock, cynical assumption. And on such a firm basis I was prepared to conjecture.

'So we have to assume that it was worth everyone's while to hold that party. Someone was paying Charlie, in drugs or hard cash, to do it. And Nicola was paid to be there because she had to take the girl along with her. And the girl had to be there because she had to be murdered.

'You see the cunning of it, don't you? The party was created for the girl – that's what Nicola meant. It's a perfect disguise for a murder. You find a dead girl in the aftermath of a party and you draw the obvious conclusion – that she was killed accidentally, in its course. A rape, a little too much enthusiasm – something like that. You think that the murder happened at the party, whereas in fact the party happened at the murder. The whole thing was set up, organised and paid for for one reason and one reason only – to provide the circumstances of her death.'

'And if you're right,' said Eth, 'who did the killing and who did the paying? And what does this scrap of paper mean?'

133

14

We carried on drinking as the pub filled up. Mysteriously, no one seemed to come in through the door. Rather, the clientele sprang up from the carpet like enigmatic mushrooms in the night – mainly middle-management engaged in the pursuit of boredom as ruthlessly as if it were a sales target. Perhaps they drew monthly graphs of the number of anecdotes they had told about the wife, the car or Majorca and presented them to their superiors for praise or blame. ('Boredom figures up again. Well done team.') Perhaps they just bored each other for the hell of it.

And on the edge of this banality I was thinking. Thinking and drinking. The two processes became so merged – so mutually diluted – that I could practically see my thoughts swilling darkly in an amber-yellow fizz; thoughts that turned slowly, recurring, serpentine, with a volition of their own.

Charlie became explicable: his strange calm, for instance, that morning after the party when he had sat placidly with a corpse in his junk room. He had known beforehand that it was due to be collected – that, surely, was part of the deal – like a receipted parcel. The fifty pounds he had given me could have been nothing other than a pay-off; a request or a warning to me, right at the start, not to get involved. His unhelpfulness, his obstructions later – they could all be entered in a ledger, balanced and accounted for with a pseudo-mathematical precision. I had been in the presence of a very smart operator and I had only just noticed the fraud.

And another thought, sinking like a ship's safe through

thick water, twisting down and never touching bottom: 'Whatsoever cometh forth of the doors of my house shall surely be the Lord's.' It sounded like a promise made between a man and his God, over the girl's head, commending her finally to his merciless care. It was a threat that she would have to return – but return to whom? It stated that her fate followed in a curve from the instant of her going to the instant of her coming back again; that it was closed, pre-empted.

So many big words attached to that portentous quotation. It towed a certain vocabulary in its wake – an exaggerated, resonant vocabulary. The mushrooms were leaving and the landlord was unplugging the fruit machines before I recognised it. It had to belong to one man. It gave off his echoes – a sound signature as individual as any handwriting.

'It has to be his,' I told Eth.

'Whose?' she demanded. 'What?'

'His,' I said, as if there could be only one Him. And I added, for clarity's sake, 'Letherbridge's.'

'How do you know?'

'I know,' I replied. 'I'm sure. It's got Him written all over it.'

'Then we'll have to go and see him,' she said.

In our silence she had been drinking as much as me – almost as if it were a political point or at least a matter of pride. I was reminded of that other evening when we had collided on our way to an identical destination. But, although I had good reason to believe she was drunk, this decree had to it the awful finality of one of Eth's decisions. I feared dreadfully that it would not be revoked in sobriety's cold morning.

Nor was I mistaken. The very next morning, at eight a.m. precisely, Eth's sharp-shoed toe prodded the belly of the sleeping bag wherein I was temporarily curled. I opened my eyes on a world still webbed by sleepiness's spider.

'When' – a long, insinuating when – 'you've got up, you can ring Willy.'

I raised my head to stare angularly at her from the floor. She was standing, her legs astride and her fists on her hips. Those familiar, forbidden thighs stretching tight the skin of a short, leather skirt. She seemed to have uncluttered herself of all sad complications. She stood above me with a simple and absolute confidence, as though created by the French Revolution or the director of a cabaret troupe. I realised that, by rights, I should have a hangover and groaned nostalgically back to the carpet's bristly pillow.

'We're going tonight,' she persisted. 'You and me and Willy.'

I made loud, hoggish snoring sounds – not so much to pretend that I was asleep as to intimate that I didn't wish to be awakened. Ineffectual.

'I'll call from work to check that you've done it. If you haven't, you'll be on the street this evening.'

And then a pause. Mittened sounds ruffled beyond my sleeping bag's hushedness. It was the sort of suspension of action when one yearns to peep out to see what the adversary's up to, but it's a matter of pride or pretence not to care. I wondered if Eth was running a bucket of cold water. Or preparing to kick me with renewed force. Or making me a cup of coffee.

It turned out to be none of these. She was only leaving. The front door's unambiguous slam told me there would be no personal engagement. I was left with the most difficult thing of all, then – no fight and her orders hovering, backed neither by violence nor blandishments, as a charge of honour. Undisobeyable.

Sulkily I slithered from the floor, like the first finny steps of a fish unwillingly complying with evolution – and set about doing those things necessary to install oneself as a human being in the new day. I dressed, washed, white-foamed last night's ashy teeth in bracing toothpaste surf. I felt that it was somehow imperative to be fully up – to be civilised, even – before ringing Willy. I meant it as a tribute to his formal qualities.

I got through without any difficulty. Perhaps, like God, he was always accessible in time of need – no matter how far we have strayed.

'It has been some time, Mr Paris,' he reproached.

'A day or two,' I confessed; and began lavishly to recite the adventurings, the discoveries, the connections that had led us – proleptically – to Letherbridge's door.

Willy, of course, was silent throughout my narration. But, when I told him about the dedication and how I had divined its authorship, his silence audibly deepened. I could sense him on the other end of the line, his motionless face carved with impassive intelligence, absorbing what I said so utterly that the words no longer felt as though they belonged to me. He had taken the responsibility of them to his safer heart.

After I'd finished there was such a protracted quiet that I thought I'd lost him. Eventually he asked, 'You have not misremembered this quotation?'

'No,' I assured him. 'That's it. Exactly.'

'My father was a very religious man,' he said. 'He preached to me on many occasions. This stirs a portion of memory.'

'You recognise it then?'

'Perhaps,' he replied. 'It is very serious matter – to recognise a quotation such as this.' Another pause. His deliberations seemed to me like the slow settling of a ball on a roulette wheel. Then, 'I shall come this evening,' he determined.

It rained throughout the day. Sometimes a deluge, sometimes a desultory drizzle, but it never stopped altogether, so that the drumming or the dribbling on the rooftops played in my head like a subtle, unending jazz rhythm. I spent the time thinking, lounged at full stretch on Eth's red and black sofa – which was, vexingly, exactly the wrong length. If my head was couched comfortably in a cradle of cushions, my legs had to angle upwards over the far arm like a pair of fishing rods stuck by a stream. Conversely, if I reeled in my feet, my neck was propped against the near arm's hard edge. I rearranged myself every quarter of an hour.

And I smoked continuously. As one who dislikes used ashtrays I emptied mine frequently, extracting the butts first and then distributing the lizard shit detritus amongst Eth's indoor plants, crumbling pinches of it into each pot with a beneficent, priestly air. Incanting in Latin as I dappled my green congregation with grey.

Linda began to flitter through my mind again. At first it was no more than that – a bat's wing brush in a cobwebbed room, or a figure passing lightly and softly across the distant end of a corridor. A footfall, a presence, and then only the softest imprint of a presence like a shadow in the air. Soon she began to stay a little longer – to loiter, as though she expected to meet someone. And, shortly after that, she was always standing there. She wasn't the girl I had expected her to be.

Her eyes; her pale blue eyes. They seemed to have been switched off, like a neon sign unlit during daytime. Her lips lurched to one side in a sneer of stupefaction. Perhaps she had sneered once and then the wind had changed, fixing her for ever with that expression, so that even when she was being killed her face at least would have registered nothing more than a dull disdain for the process.

I had to place her in a room – not the one I had first invented, where a fatly sentimental landlady baked in a tiled kitchen. The one, instead, that I'd seen – with the landlord wheezing below and Nina twitching above. She had existed in that naked room between two thinnesses, as if she were a sand-dune between sand-dunes, diminished by the wind.

She was going to a party and she was neither happy nor unhappy. This was, after all, in the line of business. There

138

had probably been some financial enticement. She was merely going to work – performing a series of Monday morning actions, early that Saturday evening, with sleep-ridden sullenness. And this time I saw everything; saw her in the bathroom staring at her flesh. She was plucking at it like a housewife disapproving of a grocer's chicken.

In the mirror slanted above the sink, splashing its silver square on the ceiling, she could not see all of herself; only a slice, from the shoulders upward, contemplating herself as though she were a newly met stranger with whom she had few affinities. The girl who looked into the mirror was wondering how she had become the girl who looked out of the mirror. She was trying to determine by what sudden fall or by whose opaque decree she had become one of Willy's girls – as if what had happened to her had occurred in some lacuna of consciousness, or as if she had sleepwalked into slavery, waking in a cold country amidst alien hands.

I watched her stepping out of and into clothes. I was prepared to treat her differently this time – more zoologic-ally; to observe her as she knelt to the floor, almost in the posture of a runner on her marks, gathering up a discarded garment. Her spine climbed arched beneath the skin like a mountain railway line. The wrinkle-rippled sole of her left foot was vertical to the linoleum and, under the lightbulb's interrogatory glare, her leg from calf to upper thigh seemed to be carved in butter. An edible, salt-sweet sculpture.

I revolved her, as if she were on a turntable, gently until she faced me. Now she was crouched before me, one hand clawing out to assemble underwear and balancing herself also. It was a curiously unmuscular arm, moulded in one piece bumped outwards at the elbow. Her breasts were small and teasing gravity, with a blue bruise spreading. Looking up, her blonde hair disarranged and ashy at the roots like singed straw, she was definitely a fallen angel. She reminded me instantly of that poster of Debbie Harry – drawing-pinned above my bed – where the singer screamed upward from a scarlet stage.

139

I spun her and let her go. Watched her as she rose and crossed the landing to her bedroom. I suspected that the landlord lingeringly stared for such moments from the bottom of the staircase, his yellow-flecked cranium floating crabbish in the gloom, his tiny eyes scanning for a hint of pubic pleasure. Hints curling into shadows for him to elaborate later with his horny hand. And Linda had already passed over and was sitting underclothed at her chest of drawers, on which was propped a further mirror.

She tipped her make-up out of a dust-pink bag. It scattered with a diffuse clatter and those catatonic eyes gazed until the last lipstick had rolled and settled. Squidge-ended crayons, coagulated varnish scabbed on the sides of small bottles, truncated pencils and powder-clouded puffs. She selected colours unsuited to her, and lidded her eyes the shade of cloyed verdigris, doing it with repressed, accurate violence. It was like watching an artist slicing at her palette with a knife, or as if she were setting out not to adorn but to mutilate herself.

She painted a Pharaonic mask across her face, so that her face became a hollow mould between her and the world. It wasn't a disguise any more than the tragic or comic mask of a player in a Greek theatre was a disguise – more a strategy to indicate a fixity of attitude; perhaps to announce that she had no pity for herself. She parted her tameable hair down the centre then killed it with gel. It descended flatly past her cheeks and terminated without motion between jawbone and shoulder.

She considered her head from a forensic distance – as if the mirror were a fridge where it lay bodyless. Her fingers were upraised like candles and flickering on either side of her brow. She lacked the courage quite to touch this thing. Her hands collapsed into her lap but the face stayed stiff.

And then she began to dress. I went to the wardrobe with her and accompanied her as she tugged at the coathangers and guided her as she chose: a white dress with red, green and orange circles, white tights, a pair of scarlet shoes.

I had tried often to recall what she had really been wearing that night; but the exact details eluded me. The fact was that the rust-brown blood and the posture of her arm had been – were still – so vivid that everything else had simply faded out. She was expressed in my memory only as a twisted limb and a splash or two of colour – like a piece of mixed media art glimpsed at the ICA. Resolutely sweet, she was, and almost like a child. She was going to a party.

I sent her out on to the streets – a hybrid creature. That Egyptian head, metallic and severe, on a body clothed as if it aspired only to jelly and ice-cream. I followed her, watching her metronomic handbag – also white – tick off the rhythm of her steps. Her ankles clipping the pavement with the speed and the regularity of a sewing machine. She was going again to the tube, and this time I was determined to follow her all the way.

We stood together on the platform. I sat opposite her in the carriage. I had seen her now: seen her out of and in this costume. I had considered her with a gaze which was practically surgical in its rigour; and yet, I had failed. Failed to anatomise her. Failed to penetrate the silence. She seemed shut in a glass cell where all her actions were public but somehow enigmatic – as though she were performing a mime without a subject, or a charade, with neither the intention nor the hope of conveying meaning.

I still didn't know where she had come from. She had seemed respectable – both Willy and Nina had said so. And, being respectable, it must have been her conception of duty which had thus far saved her. She had stuck to it. She had behaved like a princess – a fairytale figure, plummeting till she landed on the milkmaid's stool; displaced from the palace but retaining all the while that quality essential to a palace existence – an unflinching acceptance of the etiquette of things, which occasionally passed itself off as dignity or grace.

I still wasn't near her, though. I wondered how I could get closer – close enough to understand. I wanted to tear

141

away appearances – to strip her down beyond her clothes – to flay her alive, as it were; as though turning back the overlayed pages of a medical textbook, each one revealing a more secret intestinal entwinement.

I had already emptied the carriage. I had foreordained that this should be an intimate encounter. It was proving convenient. I only had to halt the train on some fabulous pretext. I only had to fuck her surprisingly, against her will.

I've always maintained that it's impolite to wank in one's hostess's sleeping bag. No matter with what preventative care one deploys handkerchief or tissues, inaccuracy and seepage treacherously collude to deposit a detectable glob – as surely as one will soak oneself when wrestling with a splurging hosepipe. Consequently, in my exile at Eth's, I had accumulated a backlog of orgasms demanding to be dealt with like unanswered mail. It may have been this milkshake froth which bubbled me into fantasy. It may have been a loftily Lawrentian conviction in the soul-searing powers of screwing. Whatever it was, I began to dream myself raping her.

I couldn't seduce her and it would have been pointless to buy her. And it had to be brutal, without being so brutal that it hurt. In fact, a rape by mutual consent.

She kicked off her shoes. Front of foot to back of foot, and flip. A challenging, bed-edge gesture. She raised herself slightly in the seat and drew that juvenile dress up to her waist; began rolling down her tights with palms pressed straight against her thighs. Rolled them down and down, bringing her knees up right below her chin and disengaged them from her toes as delicately as if she were removing a splinter. They contracted on the floor like a chalk-scrawled figure of eight, knickers enmeshed within.

But this was incidental. I was watching her face – her ancient, green-gilded face. I was scrutinising it in expectation of a telling change, and what I saw appalled me. It wasn't her sneer – I had grown accustomed to that. It was those unlit eyes, suddenly sparked with tubular electricity like the first flicker in a shop window before business commences.

She was coming towards me, her hem uplifted. She halted, standing with that repulsed, fastidious poise of someone stepping through uncertain mud. She straddled my lap and I suspected an intimation of dampness passing osmotically through my membraneous jeans – although it may merely have been the fancy of a hypochondriac seeking perspiration on his own brow. Belt buckle wrenched back. Quick tightness then tongue and pin flapping loose. Stud and fastener separated and zip's lips unlingeringly parted. Her twinned hands preparedly turned back my underpants, with the motion of a servant turning back a guest-room counterpane.

I was engaged in a sexual act with a girl who was, after all, dead. Her fingers pinched and slid as if they were performing a prelude to torture – as if she were assessing, for future reference, the exact point at which pleasure crossed over to pain. I wanted to take her by the haunches and heave her round. To knot a fistful of hair in my hand and have her from behind, stabbing alternate orifices. To judder come amid her parted arse. Withdraw and let it drip, ammoniac.

I shuddered with a sort of snake-skin shedding shrivel into consciousness; suffering the slight dizziness of incipient hyperventilation. Peered over the side of Eth's sofa with foreboding – like a mountaineer peeping into a crevasse for a swallowed comrade. I discovered that I was connected to my ashtray by a spider's milky thread, and in the ash a plasmic sprawl had flopped. I blessed the intelligent jelly and began to speculate whether or not it would be good for the plants.

That evening, as we waited, Eth fretted. She drank coffee from small cups and smoked a fraction of half a dozen cigarettes. She was afflicted by a kind of backstage nervousness, suspended in a fractured time when one series of

143

events has played itself out and another has yet to begin.

'What will we say to him?' she asked. 'What will we do?'

'We ask him what he wants with a dead body,' I replied, and carried on gargling whisky, noisily.

I was quite drunk and it was nearly midnight when Willy arrived. Eth let him in and he entered and stood in the middle of the lounge, rain-flecked fedora unremoved, clearing his cataracted glasses with a silk handkerchief. He was breathing heavily after his ponderous dash from car to door.

'The rain will cease tonight,' he assured us. 'This downpour will be the last. The sky will be empty but the ground will be soft.'

'So what?' I enquired.

'I have brought a spade.'

'Good idea,' I said. 'Which one?' And immediately wished I hadn't.

Willy turned his spectacles on me, as indifferent as a surveillance camera. 'Tonight, Mr Paris, for your stupidity, you shall dig.'

15

The sky had closed down low and flat like a mahogany lid over our heads. A stranded dampness hung wispy and invisible in the air like a loose eyelash, touching and unfound. And we stood around the grave – the three of us – apparently wondering what it would be appropriate to think or feel. Willy had removed his hat. Eth was shrunk deep into her coat. And I – I was leaning on my spade. I had a job to do.

I saw no point in reverence or respect. Either would have been like the deceitful politeness of the hangman. We had, after all, come to dig her up. It seemed distinctly wrong to sanctify her with silent prayer. She was dreadfully material. We were going to use her for a purpose.

There was a coffin-shaped mound of earth at our feet. I had kicked away the obscuring leaves to reveal it, and criss-crossed on it were the bootprints of a deliberate man. The savage engravings of a god we were very close to.

We were at the bottom of a garden. Five slender firs, persuasive as a woman's long fingers, barred us from the lawn. We were in the hidden place of stones with damp undersides, of worms and light-loathing beetles; where a bonfire had been and where the compost heap still was – orange skins, grass, leaves, the tops and tails of carrots impacted into black, organic slabs. They had been compressed into a sort of parodic cake, so thick it could have been sliced. And here she was buried, between ashes and waste, as Willy had unerringly known she would be.

In the car – Eth in the front seat next to Willy, sitting rigid with the pioneering fanaticism of someone who saw only the end of a journey and not its intermediate vicissitudes; me in the back like an inebriate but indispensable guide – Willy had said –

'I have done my homework. Frequently I enjoin my son Samuel to do his; it would be inconsistent of me, therefore, if I did not do mine.'

'What?' I asked. 'Why? Wherefore? When?'

'You are drunk, Mr Paris. All this will happen and it will pass you by. It will mean nothing to you.'

'Sod the meaning,' I advised him. 'Just tell me what we're doing.'

'With the aid of an address book provided by the man Mick, I examined your Mr Letherbridge's house this afternoon. I located, without difficulty, the grave of my dead girl.'

'Yes? Where does that leave us?'

'We are going' – Willy articulating with the teeth clench-ing clarity of a man barely restraining himself from violence or tears – 'to disinter her body.'

'Then stop the car;' I ordered, my fists thumping down on the back of Willy's seat like a child pummelling a giant uncle's chest. The joke had gone too far. The car remained unperturbed, its speed neither increasing nor diminishing. But it felt as though it was rolling with the accumulated momentum of that hearse which I had dreamed that night in the Pacific, when Eth had given a simple answer to a simple question.

'The car does not stop,' Willy decreed. He habitually made his commonplaces sound like universal truths. 'I am an old man, full of impatience. I have no longer any time to be troubled. I must go straight to the heart of things. I have decided that we will finish this matter tonight.'

'Why this way?' I persisted. I wasn't disconcerted by the illegality of what was proposed, and certainly not by its immorality. We had been functioning – all of us – too long in something as childishly fair as a treasure hunt for that to be of consequence. If the grown-ups had seen us rupturing their hedges, they certainly weren't bothered. It was the messiness lying ahead that disturbed me: the rain-weighed earth pyramided on a blistering spade; the opened grave growing bigger, sides funnelling down and crumbs of dirt tumbling antish to the bottom; the spade's blade prying a picked carcass from the clay.

We were out of the city now, and in the wider eeriness of suburbia. In the stagnant night I nevertheless had a sense of air sluicing through gaps – the gaps between houses, the gaps in the fences, the gap between street and tarred sky, as if there were a perpetual blowing circulating in the empti-ness. It was the restless turning of a night that couldn't sleep. And the passing streetlamps paled Eth's profile intermittently, blanking her out then lighting her orange-pink again, as though I were watching only every other frame of a film.

'Why this way?' I repeated.

'We have no evidence,' said Willy. 'I know everything but I can prove nothing.' And then he added inconsequentially, soliloquially, almost, 'Besides, I am as great a man as he.'

Just as Willy had known the rain would stop so he had found the grave. And, when I asked him how that was, he grunted, 'The workings of this man are plain to me.' It was as if he were ascribing his knowledge not to accumulated facts or hazarded calculations but to an occult equivalence between himself and that other one. It was as if they were merely opposites, or two sides of the same coin.

Perhaps they had balanced each other, measured each other, watched and shadowed each other to the point where they could replicate each other in thought and deed. As if Willy knew because he nearly was.

'Is she buried deep?' I asked.

'Deep,' Willy echoed, his voice exaggerating cavernously.

I stabbed the ground savagely and flicked a spadeful of dirt at his ankles. Soft earth, loosely parcelled round her. I dug out the surface of the coffin shape, throwing the earth out wildly so that Willy and Eth had to hop hither and thither to avoid it.

'He's doing it deliberately,' Eth complained.

'He is in a sulk,' Willy explained. 'My son, Samuel, similarly dislikes working.'

Then they withdrew, and I dug and dug in silence. Occasionally I looked up to confirm that they were still there. Squat blacknesses, identifiable amongst other blacknesses. Eth was stiff and tutting, impatient at my toils; and Willy's silhouette was somehow – I noticed it – curiously expectant – like a man who has lit a firework, retreated, and waits for the overdue explosion.

Eth's Scotch, which had imparted such courageous energy to my early labours, was starting to wear off and a wholly rational fear was replacing it – fear like black coffee, iced. It began to seem to me that this feeling, far from being a wild cry in the heart's hollow hall, was the reasonable result of lucidity's onset. Ghost stories recited themselves in my mind. I hung out signals telling them to stop, but it was as if my memory were a station platform on which I had to stand. Narratives clattered through like unwanted trains. I remembered hands that had sprung like sudden tulips from the soil; embraces in putrid arms, loving me to hell; dead mouths with other worldly invitations. The tawdry pay-offs of old paperbacks had begun to whisper to me with irrepressible reality.

I heard Eth murmur to Willy, 'Will she come back? Do you think she'll answer us? After she's been gone so long?'

And Willy muttered, 'My people have a saying – "The hair of the wicked turns white." We have many legends to account for this phenomenon.'

If it had been a Sunday afternoon, replete with the trivial details of solidified existence, I would have mocked their hushed cathedral tones. But, thigh-deep in a grave, my skull like a catacomb where every toestep stumbled on a bone, I stupidly hissed, 'You're trying to frighten me.' A wire of words strung out on a high, high pitch.

The earth squirmed turbulent beneath me. Shiny worms dived. I realised there was a tear of sweat trembling hotly on my eyelid. I wiped it away and struck down again. Terror was expanding inside me like a balloon being inflated. I saw that it was a sky-blue colour and I foreknew that soon there would be nothing but terror. I would be a taut-stretched bag of tension, ready to burst. Shallow breath squeezed into the corners of my lungs.

I struck down with the spade once again and felt the momentary resistance of something ligamentous and snappable jarring up to the handle. I dared to look to where the spade had struck and saw, adhering to it, severed by it, a brown crooked finger.

The final pinprick piercing the skin. Blue, ragged edges –

saliva-slicked and torn – slapping on each other with a coronary palpitation. Collapsed arse-first in the soil, my diaphragm hiccuping huge sobs through a constricted throat.

I sat there for a long time, listening to the sobs subside. Willy came over and bent into the hole. He picked out a four-inch fragment of tree root, surgically sliced, and showed it to me.

'You have made a lot of noise,' he said, 'over this. Stand up and see. The damage is done.'

His hands under my armpits, hauling me up. My legs still wanted to fold themselves away like the rickety struts of a card table. He turned me to face the rear of the house where the light in the kitchen had been switched on. A middle-aged man in white pyjamas and a white flannel dressing gown was swigging milk straight from the bottle.

When he had finished drinking he reached towards a shelf above him. He took down a key and came to the back door. His shape shivered geometrically behind the frosted glass. He opened the door and came walking across the lawn, his slippers flapping on and off his heels. It was the man we had referred to simply as the man, the stone man, or the Stone Age man; who had come to stand for some immense, civilised barbarity – a deity graven in rock, the silent dispenser of punishment for unseen sins; who now plodded across the lawn with the common tetchiness of any woken husband and said –

'My wife's a light sleeper.'

'I was not deterred,' said Willy.

'I would have followed you,' Eth declared, 'to the ends of the earth.' Letherbridge raised his eyebrows heavily and slowly at her. It was the only indication he was to give that he had met her before.

'It was fucking hard work,' I added.

We were at a disadvantage. We had to account for ourselves. We had been caught in an act that was positively naughty. We were like children who had climbed over the wall and into the ogre's garden. According to legend he was wicked and fierce, the jealous guardian of his fruit. But, peering at him from behind the trees, defaced by the fir needles' dense scribble, he reminded me of a glob of lard rapidly melting in a frying pan. Perhaps it was his leprous whiteness. Perhaps it was the soft edges of his recent sleepiness. Whatever it was, though, he didn't seem dangerous.

'She's in there all right,' he told us. 'But I don't know what you'd have found. It's been three weeks.'

Then we stood there, behind our partial screen, waiting for something to happen. This was meant to be the final confrontation. We had trespassed. We had provoked. We had brought the man to us and we were strangely confounded. It wasn't the enormity of his presence – he was hardly the god we'd expected. It was, in fact, quite the reverse; we were confounded by his mild vulnerability – as though, at the very heart of darkness, we had found – instead of Mistah Kurtz – a misunderstood philanthropist, the victim of malicious gossipings.

'Won't you go away?' he asked. 'Now you know? Now I've admitted it?'

'What have you admitted?' I returned, glad to have a ball to toss.

He shrugged. 'That she's there.'

'It's not enough,' said Eth, who always wanted more. She had been told something that was too small for her to believe in. 'Why is she dead? How did she get there? What's going to become of her?'

'Let's just leave it,' he answered. 'Go home. Forget it. Pretend it never happened.'

'Fine,' I concurred. 'Let's do that.'

'No,' Willy, gritting the glazed path of my ambitions.

'No,' Eth, whispering defiance at the scandal. She had felt the girl slipping away, as if rescuing her were an operation carried out across ice-floes in a crystal sea. Their fumbling arms had met and – no matter what the numbness in the hand or the coldness in the bones – she wasn't going to let go. 'There's a hole in the ground. I want to know what went into it. I want the story that was buried with it.'

'Ah,' Letherbridge shrugged again. It was the sort of gesture that communicates to a foreigner that she can't be understood – let alone helped. He gave us a smile – weak – a little splash of sympathy. There was nothing more he could do. 'I must be getting back to my wife,' he said. 'She'll be wondering what's happened to me.'

And he was truly going. I thought it was all over. I thought it was ending with a grave that was neither filled nor unfilled and with this man's vague assurance that there was something at the bottom of it.

Beside me, in the darkness, I could hear Eth incanting, 'Make him stay. Make him stay' – as if he were a fairy manifestation who might grant us wishes. But I had no way of making him stay and I was aware, moreover, that the gods often punish mortals by granting their wishes too completely. I didn't want to hear the truth. I wanted a bath. I wanted to sleep between clean sheets.

And Letherbridge was turning and, in that instant, my perception changed. He didn't turn like a husband going back to bed. He turned like a coward who had triumphed. His shoulders dropped with the relief of a man walking away from a fight. His steps were fractionally quick for someone who was merely weary. It was a mistake I had seen before: a bad actor, keen to be offstage, dropping out of character on his way to the exit.

Willy must have seen it too. He broke through the branches like a wild boar. He even grunted. His thick legs pounded the grass and his unsuitable body had the forward wobbliness of a baby's. He charged – or, possibly, collapsed on to – Letherbridge – and they rebounded off each other and to the lawn with a playpen comicality.

Willy got up first. He collected his hat – which had been thrown like a knight unseated in a joust – and inspected it

151

as though it were the outward and visible sign of his dignity. It was not much damaged. It had suffered only temporary indentations. He sighed and glanced sideways at Eth and me, who had ventured out on to the grass. 'My son, Samuel, is attempting to master the art of rugby,' he explained. 'He has demonstrated several techniques to me.'

Letherbridge had re-erected himself also. He seemed to have hauled himself into place. He stood, shamelessly statuesque, in the centre of the garden. He had assumed what I had always imagined to be his true identity. The moon had colluded with him, waiting until this metamorphosis before giving him a pencil line of light in which to stand. His flannel gown with its folds was now monumentally sculpted. Grey shadows fountained around him.

His black lips wriggled, touched with disgusting animation, like the slow stirrings of a pair of slugs. 'Come inside,' he invited us.

'What will you say to your wife?' I asked.

'My wife?' – searching for her like a pebble fallen amongst pebbles – 'Oh. She hears nothing. She's a heavy sleeper.'

16

The kitchen's fluorescent light changed him again. This time he had a dusty, limestone look. I feared that he was riven by internal cracks – that he would crumble or gradually be diminished by a draught, his voice reducing to a whisper as he blew away, and failing altogether on the final words – whatever they might prove to be.

He began solidly enough, though. He said, 'There's a dead girl at the bottom of my garden. So what?'

Big silver spoons and a set of scalene carving knives hung behind his head. The room was impregnated with the old odours of mince and pork and Sunday beef and boiled potatoes with everything. He had set his bottle of milk in front of him and its pale spoor curved to the rim where he had sipped at it. We were sitting – the four of us – round a table and we could have been about to play cards.

'I shall tell you why we are here,' said Willy. He spread his hands out flat along the table's edge, as if to smooth away any rumples of misunderstanding. 'My friend, Angelo, has a piece of paper which he believes to have been authorised by you. It would seem that you are implicated, by your own hand, in unbecoming deeds. Mr Paris, show him the paper.'

'I've got it,' said Eth unclasping her handbag and fumbling obediently inside. She withdrew the fateful, quartered scrap and unfolded it, then held it out at arm's length, holding it top and bottom as though it were a scroll.

Letherbridge stared with the salt-sprayed eyes of a crow's nest sailor – grey eyes, matching the unremitting sea. His milk-blanched lips slid on his face like shitting snow as he admitted, 'Ah, yes. I recognise the handwriting.'

'You might as well confess,' Eth threatened stoutly. 'We know everything.'

'A few bits here and there we'd like clearing up,' I qualified.

He looked at us wearily, like a chemistry teacher dealing with exceptionally dull children. 'The technique,' he advised, 'is for the interrogator to know half. Half. That way you can check what you're told against what you're sure of. See if it fits. I'm trying to help you.'

He stood up abruptly. His right hand, in his dressing gown pocket, was fiddling with something. His hidden fingers were knotting and unknotting themselves like a nest of baby snakes. 'I could tell you, of course. That would be easy enough. But then – how would you believe me? You must find out for yourselves. You must' – he emphasised the word – 'verify. You've got to ask me questions.'

'In the manner of scientific enquiry?' I suggested.

'If you like. Forensic. What would you say to a cup of tea?'

'This is a very British solution,' said Willy. 'There are other technologies which are more efficacious.'

'And let's sit somewhere more comfortable. It gets chilly in here at night.'

'You're a murderer,' Eth protested. 'We can't drink tea with you.'

'Come on. He's not going to poison us.'

'That's the spirit,' Letherbridge urged. 'Give me the benefit of the doubt.'

His hand relaxed from its clandestine pastime. He filled the kettle, as it were, encouragingly. He was trying to jolly us along.

I was seeing him in close-up for the first time and he appeared to be – there was no other word for it – affable. Only once, for that statuesque moment in the garden, had he conformed to my expectations. Then he had been truly terrifying – the monolithic monster I had anticipated. I put it down to a trick of the light. The treacherous moon had briefly tainted him.

And yet, I reminded myself, he had committed crimes. His thuggery towards Nina; at one remove, my bomb; and, at an even shadier remove, he was responsible for the girl's death. It was as if he was a *trompe-l'œil* drawing – one by Escher, perhaps – in which two quite distinct impossibilities were concealed.

He arranged four cups, four saucers, milk and sugar on a silver tray. 'Given to me,' he explained, slowly swilling water round the teapot, 'when I left Manchester. I was in the vice squad there. But you know that. You know everything.'

'Prostitution,' cried Eth, connecting joyfully.

'Not really,' he replied. 'More pornography. They're very solitary people, the Mancunians.'

He carried on rocking the teapot in his massive hands – a motion he seemed simply to have forgotten to terminate whilst he gazed at the ceiling. 'It puts you off the human body, that deluge of flesh. No. Let me be precise, since it's a true confession you're after. It's the female body it revolts you from. It looks different on paper. Shinier.' He turned to Eth, as though his own irony had sneaked up and surprised him. 'We're both Puritans, after all, you and I. Shall we go through to the lounge?'

We followed in a timid crocodile: him, me, Eth, Willy. Down the hallway's treacly light. He had indicated, conspiratorial finger and a mimed 'shhh', that he desired silence – or as much of it as was possible. I found myself banging into things. A glass cabinet tinkled. A grandfather clock gave off a wooden burp from deep in its hollow stomach. Eth hissed and kicked me on the ankle.

Letherbridge entered the unlit room before us. Standing on the threshold, I heard the crockery chatter and fall still – deposited on a table in his familiar territory. Then the orange-blossom light unfolded brightly and I saw Letherbridge with his hand to the switch innocently unaware that what he had revealed was sensational.

Circled in the middle of the floor, looping behind armchairs and diverting under the full length of the sofa, its complex siding criss-crossed beside the patio window, was the most elaborate model railway I had ever seen. A multitude of engines – maroon and gold, olive-green, black, blue and yellow – painted in pristine matt dullness, stood stationary with their attendant carriages. They had a miniaturised dignity to them, laughable if it hadn't been so deadly serious, like a dwarf in a dinner suit. There were small, rural stations, their personnel poised forever in the conduct of precise business; and three signal boxes, each manned by a dummy eternally vigilant in his fresh uniform. On a papier-mâché hill sweeping up beside a stretch of track, a black-clad figure shared a picnic with a girl in a primrose dress.

'I set it up at midnight,' said Letherbridge. 'And I dismantle it just before dawn.'

Eth, all eagerness and elbows, was crowding at my shoulder, trying to see what had made me halt in such wonderment. No doubt, she expected some macabre treat – a rotten corpse in a winding sheet, or a gallery of instruments of torture, perhaps. I stood aside to let her look.

Personally, I found his train set beautiful and rather touching. Quite apart from an atavistic urge to play with it myself, I was relieved to discover that – if Letherbridge was mad at all – it was a madness writ small. He was prey to a childish foible – something tender, like a deep cut gained in an accident. But Eth, with that ruthlessness towards human nature which habitually characterises fanatics, that deliberate excision of anything sentimental, snarled –

'Toys for the boys.' (She had once referred me to a feminist psychoanalytic textbook – *Orgasms in Space*, Nellie Nile, Essex University Press, q.v. – which proved that, where men were concerned, everything was a substitute for masturbation. Truly, a seminal work.)

Willy, meanwhile, had stopped and selected one of the engines. He held it with gentle curiosity, as if it were something he had always hoped would exist, running its wheels over the back of his hand. 'This is admirable,' he murmured. 'It is executed with much deliberation.' He replaced it delicately on the rails and propelled it manually round a bend.

Letherbridge was watching us with a connoisseur's calculation – measuring, I suspected, the exact extent of his collection's effect on us. He was certainly satisfied – at least with Willy's and my response. But there was something less than naïve about his restless gaze. It struck me that he was looking for a secondary response – not merely the effect, but the effect of the effect. His heart had not gone out to us.

'My wife doesn't like it,' he said. 'That's why I can only use it during the hours of darkness.'

'She's real, then?' I asked. I was beginning to have my doubts about the palpability of the situation. I felt, oddly, that it might have been created specially for us; that it was a fairy castle charmed from the air for our delusion.

'Oh yes.' His right hand went into his pocket again and jumped instantly out. He sucked his fingertips, as though they had been burnt. 'I have a photograph here. Taken at our wedding.'

He lumbered over to the sideboard, picking his huge feet, his flapping slippers, carefully over the lines. He took up a framed picture and thrust it out towards the three of us. He seemed unsure precisely to whom he should offer it and it stayed, suspended in his grasp, for general inspection.

Willy remained unmoved. Eth shied away with a moralistic snort, like a horse confronted with unacceptable oats. I alone ventured forward to examine it. It showed the shape of the future Letherbridge. He stood with a four-square, full frontal awkwardness, perhaps not quite accustomed to his own body's bulk, carrying it like an armoured shell. He was wearing one of those forties suits, cut in such a way that it appeared to have been stitched together from squares and triangles. He clasped his bride to him with a clumsy possessiveness that took no account of her comfort. He seemed to be half lifting her and half folding her – as though her waist were merely a kind of hinge.

The girl herself reminded me of a chicken hung upside down. Brainless bewilderment was atrophied on her small features. She was dressed, not in white, but pale blue.

'There was a lot of rationing then,' said Letherbridge. 'It was just after the war.'

'Why,' asked Willy, taking a step further into the room, 'are you telling us about your wife?'

'She's a very remarkable woman,' he replied. 'Clean and tidy. Sometimes she bites her lip.' He tapped his lower lip with his forefinger.

157

'But, the girl,' Eth insisted. 'We want to know about the girl.'

'Tea!' Letherbridge cried. 'I'd completely forgotten that.'

The three of us sat down. We were going to be kept waiting for some time. Eth and I on the sofa, Willy expanding exactly to fill the available armchair.

The room itself was predominantly brown, tempered with gold; the curtains hanging straight like tree trunks and the wallpaper knotched and whorled. The carpet was densely autumnal. We could have been in an oak-panelled study or at the heart of a thick forest – I wasn't quite sure which. I felt myself to be in a constricted space and in the open air simultaneously, as though the room was constantly turning itself inside out. I supposed that the sprawling train set had something to do with the sensation: a vast geography shrunk to small proportions.

Letherbridge didn't offer us tea in the conventional manner. His simian arm shot a cup and saucer at each of us. And we got milk and sugar, whether we wanted it or not.

'Biscuits,' he proposed. 'I've got police biscuits, if you'd care to try them.'

'Police biscuits?' I queried.

'Oh yes.' He was briefly animated, staring at me, his eyes sparking with the crystalline dazzle of excitement. 'They're the same as ordinary biscuits, but they have the stamp of authority on them.'

'I think not,' said Eth, primly.

I was beginning to wonder if these wildly flaunted eccentricities were a ploy on his part – if he was pretending to a genial brand of madness in order to deflect the pointed allegations we were bound to bring against him. Playing God's fool before the court. There was, however, the intractable matter of the model railway. That must have been set up before we arrived, bearing witness to a genuine oddity of character. For there was no way he could have known we were coming. Surely.

158

'We are here to conduct business,' said Willy. 'You have killed an item of my property.'

'A member of the international sisterhood,' said Eth.

'A girl,' I appended, putting things in perspective.

Letherbridge was sitting now, to my left, his chair at an angle such that he could face Willy and me equally. His hands, clasped, dropped between his knees, where his dressing gown provided a sort of hammock for them.

'I want you to understand,' he began, 'what drives a man. What makes a man behave. I want to appeal to you – as fellow human beings.'

It was as if he was tapping us, each in turn, to see if we would emit a common chord. He looked up at us, his eyes only slightly too narrow to be fully pleading. We said nothing.

'Cleaning,' he explained. 'It goes on all around me. She dusts. She polishes. She eradicates dirt.'

'You want to blame your wife?' I asked. I was trying to get hold of a line, a thread, we could pursue.

'No.' Firmly. 'I blame the triangle. The arrangement of relationships. We were a very close family. You see' – he pointed – 'on that hillside. My daughter and myself.'

We glanced at the tiny couple, allowed each night to share a picnic from a hamper not as large as a fingernail; then back to him.

'We used to go on outings together. My wife always stayed behind. She took the opportunity to clean the house. It was a long time before I understood the meaning of this. I've always been a very stupid man. Slow to grasp things.'

Slow to grasp things – it seemed a provocative jest, because he couldn't possibly have been as slow as us. Of all the connections – thinkable and unthinkable – that might have existed between a senior policeman and a young prostitute, it had turned out to be the cosiest. The one closest to home.

'So she was –' Eth gasped, dramatically incomplete. Her

159

voice had risen to a scandalised pitch.

'Your daughter,' I callously completed.

'You killed your daughter.'

But Letherbridge seemed incapable of replying. His hand was buried again, clutching in his pocket. He withdrew it, clenched around his secret fetish. He was grinning, like a child about to reveal a mouse to a nervous aunt. He hunched forward, keeping his shut fist close to him. His fingers stretched out cautiously like a curled up spider unwrapping itself. He was holding a ball bearing.

'I touch it in moments of distress,' he said. 'It gives me consolation. It's round and wholesome. You can see how tangled everything else is.'

'Put it simply,' I pressed. 'Tell us what you did.'

'I did nothing.' He answered sulkily, as if he wished, perhaps, that he had done more. 'Events surrounded me and there I was – in the middle of them.'

'Then let us elicit gradually the meaning of things.' It was Willy in his priestly mode again.

Letherbridge callipered his silver ball between finger and thumb and squinted at it. 'It's practically the same shape as the world,' he mused. 'It just needs to be squeezed a little at the poles.'

Willy rose from his seat with something of the majesty of a balloon unleashed from its terrestrial moorings. He stood, carefully, on one leg, his right foot poised in the sky above a steam engine. The driver and stoker toiled on, oblivious to the threatening, shoe-shaped cloud.

'Mr Letherbridge,' he announced, 'we have endured your childish diversions long enough. If you will not speak to us plainly I shall begin to crush your toys.'

17

It was, he told us, a very hot day. He and his daughter decided to escape the house, packed a picnic, and took a train to rural Cheshire. They sat together in a breezy carriage, she in a primrose dress, he –

'In black?' I guessed.

'No. The black came later. Retrospectively. For mourning.'

They knew where they were going. When they got off the train they crossed the wooden bridge to the far platform and then walked down a brambled path behind the station. He led, she followed; black railings to the right, a shrubby steepness rising on the left.

'We walked for about twenty minutes.' He gestured apologetically to his model. 'The room isn't big enough for me to build it all to scale. The hill was really much further away than that. I'm hoping to set it up on the lawn in summer. Do it properly.'

I suddenly realised what we had before us. This elaborate mock-up wasn't merely a plaything. It was an item essential to the policeman's trade – a reconstruction of the crime. His investigative mind compelled him, night by night, to re-enact the circumstances that had led to – had led to –

'How long ago was this?' I asked.

'Four years,' he said. 'She would have been fourteen.'

They settled on the hillside and shared their food: sandwiches, cut neatly into quarters, and cake, and lemonade for her and a bottle of white wine for him. It was, he assured us, the last time he ever drank anything alcoholic.

'We had a kind of ritual after that. I would fall asleep and she would go away and amuse herself. Wander. Sometimes she would find things of interest and bring them to me. A butterfly, a stone. She was an only child.'

'So what?' I demanded harshly.

'Well,' he stared at the palms of his hands, now blank, empty, 'if I'd been a more experienced father I might have realised she was a little too old to be playing by herself. I might have bought her pop records or a pony instead. Then the disaster might never have happened.'

'What disaster?' There was not an echo in this thin-dimensioned landscape.

He had fallen asleep. And, whilst he slept, an angel of eroticism had flown overhead. He dreamed of a girl he had seen on the train. She had been wearing a white T-shirt, greyed by perspiration at the neck, so that it looked like snow dispersing in the early thaw. Denim shorts cut upwards over the thighs, fraying in his dream to the merest threads of a triangle. Shorn, golden hair catching the sun all along her shin. She had come towards him, floating up the hill, her clothes vanishing like cirrus clouds shredded on the wind.

'And then – ' he said.

I didn't need to be told. I had had this dream myself, in its grittier, urban version.

' – she touched me. I had an – ' He nudged Willy and me, as it were, with his eyebrows.

'An erection,' suggested Eth. 'I've heard tell of them.'

'It was my daughter.' His voice was hoarse, coming from the roof of his mouth, like the cry of a man in a blocked-up cave. 'She was touching me. I opened my eyes to see her face suspended in the sky. I could feel the coldness of the shadow it cast. But the real horror of the situation was in her expression – one of premeditated, experimental wickedness. You see – ' he insisted ' – you see how I was trapped.'

He drew her down beside him, then, once she was seated, he got up and walked away – a few paces. He turned to look at her. He claimed that he intended to say 'You should be ashamed of yourself' – or some such nonsense. He realised, though, that the position was much too serious for that. Letherbridge lowered himself from his chair. He dropped on to his hands and knees and crawled to the hillside. His arm crooked out with an ape's inarticulate care and he picked up the primrose girl and tilted her this way and that, scrutinising her.

'Then it took its clothes off' – his thumbnail scratching at the dummy. 'It stretched out on the grass, leaning back, its weight on its elbows. One eye screwed shut against the steady sun, the other watching me from behind its flickering eyelashes. Her legs lengthened out towards me and I began to confuse the motion of her breasts with a bloody rhythm in my head.'

'What did you do?' I asked.

He replaced the dummy savagely on the hill. The question clearly struck him as impertinent. 'I took her home.' And again that gaze of his again, flitting from face to face.

'But you said there was a disaster,' I reminded him.

He rose from his knees, brushing them as if to remove dirt or blades of grass. The disaster happened later. In the days that followed he began to understand that he had been offered an ultimatum. He would have to love his daughter as she demanded, or not at all. She had become his unsatisfied seductress, silently clamouring, each poised movement tweaking a secret nerve. He started to fear her. One night she came to his bedroom.

'What did your wife make of all this?'

'My wife?' He swung round to face me. There was something senatorial in his attitude – dignified and corrupt. His gown was disarranged, tending to slip off one shoulder, as though by the effort of pleading. 'I noticed that she was cleaning more intensely. Even where there was nothing to clean. I used to watch her setting out the tins, the bottles, the sprays, the dusters and the rags. Biting her lip. Then she would attack an invisible stain, her arm rubbing in an inward spiral until it came to the centre, the very heart of the absent blot. Sometimes she would bite her lip so hard that it bled. A raspberry dribble on her ice-cream chin.'

'Where was she,' I persisted, 'when your daughter came into the bedroom?'

'Oh,' he waved vaguely. 'She was sleeping. Somewhere else.'

The sound of the girl shutting the door woke him. She stood there naked, with the blue-black light swilling around her as though it were guided by deep-lying currents. Streaks of shadow wrapped around her neck and lay like tidal pools in the concavities of her body. The tangled seaweed space between her thighs. Convex islands of flesh, pale and disparate in the air, her sandbanks.

'All the girls at school have one,' she whispered.

'What?' asked Letherbridge. Speaking, he weirdly felt, to something dismembered.

'A body,' she replied. 'A body and a lover.'

He switched the bedside lamp on. White shade, white bulb, a ball of crude luminosity. The gaps in his daughter filled, but the effect being to make her thinner, smaller, starker.

'It's a fact you learn when you've examined as much pornography as I have,' he informed us. 'The harder you look at something, the more disgusting it becomes.'

His torso struggled up from the sheets, so that he appeared to have the head, trunk and arms of a man, the body and legs of a bed. He reached under his hybrid self to where he had a collection of magazines. Eth laughed vitriolically.

'I was studying them with a view to prosecution,' he explained. 'It's not unusual for officers to take work home.'

He licked his thumb and began to flick. Some of the pages adhered to each other and paper women siamese-twinned, tit to tit. He was searching, he said, for an image to revolt the girl. To illustrate to her the nature of her folly. To put her off.

164

He found it. A jumble of bodies heaped together in a slaughterhouse pose, as though they had been gassed by the camera. A head with a silly smile or the tongue protruding. Organs and orifices, between splayed or folded legs, raw, red and runny. Small hairs crinkled like spiders' legs across a sweaty lip.

'This,' he said. 'This.' And tapped the picture.

'Then we'll do it in the dark,' she said. And switched the lamp off and the darkness washed around him. Liquid sewage.

She slithered astride him in that drain-dark light; two blind creatures in a tunnel. As he told us, his fingers began playing a distressed game with themselves – interlacing and unweaving, contorting, bending against the joints. His phrases were disconnected, and it was clear that he was relating an experience he had only perceived fragmentarily:

'Her nails were too long . . . she was fourteen . . . she cried out twice – at the first and at the last . . . possessed by a woman older than herself . . . it's finished . . . gave up the ghost.'

But he hadn't finished yet. He took out his silver ball and massaged it between his palms, hunched over it like a man trying to start a fire by rubbing sticks together. His eyes narrowed and he could, indeed, have been staring into flames. Hoping, in their mesmeric, momentary shapes, to find the thing that cheated him.

'The little bitch,' he hissed.

'You were taken for a bit of a ride,' I said, trying to introduce a little jocularity to the situation. I was feeling that rash of uneasiness from which we English always suffer when strangers start to unravel their inmost selves before us. That irritation in the social oyster.

'You think she was a witch,' accused Eth, her long finger extended and her hair wiggishly stiff; feminism's revenge for Judge Jeffreys. 'Men still kill witches.'

'There is another iconography here,' said Willy. 'This is a deeply Christian story.'

At the time I dismissed it as one of his profounder-than-thou comments. He could be disconcertingly like an American academic at a philosophy seminar. It was only much later that I understood how obliquely right he was.

'So why did you kill her?' I asked.

'I loved her,' he replied. 'From the cradle to the grave. And she left me. I'm going to have a cigar.'

'Loved her!' cried Judgette Jeffreys with full-volume irony. 'Don't you mean fucked her? Fucked her up? Aren't we forgetting who the victim is here?'

He crossed the room with his head dropped heavily forward, extracted a cigar from its balsa box and lit it with a clumsy lighter shaped like a genie's lamp. Breathing in and out quickly, shallowly, the cigar tip winking like a traffic signal through fog, he surveyed us.

'The longer this conversation goes on, the less you comprehend. You came here convinced that I was the villain, and now I've confused you. I'm sorry.'

'I'm not confused,' Eth contradicted unsurely, like a child in the dark insisting she wasn't frightened.

'We each love people as we think best. Depending on the ways they offer themselves to us,' he reflected.

He had shuffled his pack of personas again. Now he was holding this new face up to us – a solemn king, wearied by sadness. He was capable, it appeared, not only of discarding one self and taking up another but even of changing the room around him. Its mood had quietened or dimmed, as if he had surreptitiously touched a hidden switch. The sofa on which I was sitting lulled me like a slow parachute descent into sleep. I became aware of a humming silence in the world outside. It reminded me of lapsing into anaesthesia – willingly, unwillingly – counting backwards from ten.

'Women always know best, don't they?' he challenged Eth. 'And she was a woman.'

'She left you. She knew best then.'

'Ah, yes. The footsteps on the ceiling. She'd still be alive if she hadn't done that.'

A second possibility: perhaps it wasn't that he had changed the mood – the old seducer – but that the events he was relating bore him, like a canoe, on their shifting currents. The more complex the tale became, the more convoluted he was. Perhaps he had simply been carried through white water ravings to a drifting stillness.

He told us about the sobbing sound of footsteps on the ceiling. He had sat here, in the lounge, listening to their code tapped out above him. He had heard the unambiguous pattern of somebody packing. She must have had a suitcase open on the bed because she kept returning to the centre of the room.

Then it was over. The ending happening as, in my experience, endings always do: ineptly. I thought of one of those partial, final break-ups which had once occurred between Eth and me; when she had delivered herself of a fine piece of invective, crescendoing with ' – perfidious, idle, apathetic shit!'. Applause from Angelo, aficionado of the dramatic arts. The door slams. And, thirty seconds later Eth returned, having left the keys to her flat on the kitchen table.

She – the girl – had come into the lounge, wearing a necklace Letherbridge had given her. She intended to tear it off and throw it in his face, but it wouldn't break. She tugged and tugged and still it wouldn't break. She turned and left, the chain's white imprint on her scarlet neck.

'And that was it,' he said. 'Poof! Gone!' He exhaled a doughnut of smoke and watched its upward voyage until it became amorphous and vanished in the air.

'Just like that.' I found myself congratulating him on the symbol he had conjured up. Mute cheers for the melancholy magician.

'True love,' he meditated, not seeming to regret its passing any more than a gourmet regrets the absence of the meal he's just eaten. Savouring the taste in the juices of recollection. 'It's lit behind the heart with the neon-blue flare of a gas fire. It burns for a little, then it goes out. That's all.'

'And you had her killed,' I prompted him.

'Yes,' he acknowledged. 'That was rather unfortunate, but I had to do it for my peace of mind. I couldn't have my daughter walking around London telling everybody I'd fucked her, could I now?'

He obviously found the notion outrageously funny, because he laughed so much that he sucked a wad of cigar smoke into his lungs and the laughing and the coughing began to wrestle phlegmily beneath his ribs.

I was very tired – constantly drooping towards a doze like a rain-laden leaf, then shivering up again, briefly shaking the drops of sleepiness off.

And Eth – mysterious Eth – was surviving on anger alone. Her eyes were preternaturally clear and her whole body was almost audibly vibrant – as though, beneath the skin, a resonant wire had been roughly strummed.

Willy had unbuttoned his waistcoat and let his stomach escape. It reminded me of a jelly tipped out of its mould. Four times I saw a yawn, like the bubbles a goldfish breathes, rising up his throat. Four times he harumphed and swallowed.

The morning sky was already leaking from behind the curtains. Night's black diluted to a water-grey, streaked with the non-colour a trailing paintbrush leaves when it has been all but washed out. We heard a vacuum cleaner come on upstairs, its thin mewl sucking over the carpet, a rattle of grit in its tubular throat.

'The house is coming to life,' said Letherbridge. 'I'll have to take my train set down soon.' He had been stuck in one of his pauses – a rare trough of silence – staring at the floor between his feet. It was as if he had seen, clearly marked down there, the pattern of his life as it should have been.

'You've not got long, then. To tell us how it happened.'

He looked up from his lugubrious contemplation, relishing his private grief too much to welcome being disturbed. 'They rang me from a public call box. To confirm it had been done.'

'Who did?'

'My henchmen.' He nodded slowly. He was in agreement with himself that this, indeed, was the way it had ended.

But he was inaccurate from the outset. They turned out to be not so much henchmen as henchboys: a couple of junior policemen – one, in fact, merely a cadet. He had put money in their pockets and promises in their heads – calculating that both receptacles were more or less empty – and had told them to go and hunt his daughter down.

She had vanished into the labyrinthine city about a year ago, shortly after he had been transferred to London. The henchboys had searched for her in cheap hotels, in hostels, underneath bridges and arches. They had picked their way gingerly – like men looking for a rat behind a cupboard – through encampments of cardboard boxes, lifting a newspaper here, turning a face to the torch there. They had followed the channels of runaways and vagrants, discovering a geography above the streets which quietly mimed that of the sewers below.

At first they had only heard rumours of rumours – someone had talked to someone who had described a girl who could be the one. A tale of a shadow once seen passing on a wall. But, gradually, the whispers had become more definite until an old man's finger, trembling in the park, had pointed them to a woman who slept close by.

'No one has a record,' she said, speaking with a noticeable Latin American intonation. 'All record is lost.'

Letherbridge had fun narrating this, accompanying his accent with voluminous gestures of despair – the sort one tends to see from tragic opera singers.

'Everyone sinks,' the woman went on. 'There is no trace

of the disappeared. Not here. Not in the life to come.'

'Then one of my boys kicked her in the guts and she started talking sense. She admitted she'd been to your refuge, centre, whatever, and she'd met my daughter there. She called it Beat-the-Sea Refuge. Beatah-the-Seauh.' More gestures, as though drawing the vowels like spaghetti from between his teeth.

When they got there, though, she had already flitted to Fran's; and when they got to Fran's she had just made that last, forced transition to Willy's underworld. But, by then, they were separated from her only by a thin membrane of space and time.

'There was still, nevertheless, a problem. I had to master the actual technicalities of the killing.' Letherbridge was speaking with a new, authoritative detachment in his voice – like an experimental physicist detailing to a rapt lecture hall the obstacles he had overcome. He was about to reveal to us a significant advance in the science of murder.

'How did they do it?' I asked breath-batedly.

'Who?' He snapped at the question like a mastiff at a fly. It was clearly an irrelevance.

'Your boys,' I suggested less confidently.

'Them! I wouldn't trust them with it. They were a pair of born bunglers. I gave one of them a bomb to deliver to you – and he even messed that up.'

'Oh, yes,' I conceded. 'I'd forgotten.' Then, in fairness to his junior henchman, added, 'He delivered it all right.'

'I know,' Letherbridge said crossly. 'But I specifically told him to tell you the box was full of beer. That way you would definitely have opened it and it would have blown up in your face. It had an override mechanism, you see.'

'Ah. An override mechanism. Very clever.'

'Angelo's not worth assassinating,' Eth interrupted, meanly stealing the glory conferred on me by my status as target. 'You should have gone for me.'

'We are diverging' – Chairman Willy – 'from the topic of who destroyed my property.'

'That,' said Letherbridge, 'was a difficult choice. I had to have the right sort of accomplice because – well, do you know what gives most murderers away?'

'No,' Eth and I cried in schoolchild chorus.

'The body.' Smiles all round, as if he had told us something at once obvious and remarkable. 'When a body's found, investigations are sure to follow: autopsies, reports, coroners' inquests, evidence. Sometimes the process goes as far as naming the guilty. I wanted to avoid all that, so I looked for an accomplice who would return the corpse to me. And I would simply make it disappear.' He flourished his hands at us and then peered mischievously into his dressing gown sleeves conched along his forearms. 'I needed a very special type of person. Someone at a distance from me, whom I could trust to handle the whole affair. Someone who would accept the subtle challenge of the enterprise. Someone cunning, and yet a moral imbecile. A prestidigitator of the dead.'

We heard furniture being moved about upstairs and the vacuum sucking into the pockmarks left by the legs of beds or armchairs.

'My wife,' he apologised. 'The meaning of cleaning.' It sounded like an advertising jingle.

'What is the meaning of cleaning?' I enquired.

'Me.' And he had changed again, seeming to jump back, startled, from the question. 'I'm the dirt, the ineradicable blot, on her life. It's really me she's trying to clean away.'

'Ah. Thank you. That's that cleared up.'

We waited for him to continue, but he didn't. He was plunged into one of his crevasses of contemplation, the talismanic silver ball between his palms. His lips drily fumbled against each other, as though he were reciting a prayer.

'You lost him,' said Eth. 'Get him back.'

I snapped my fingers twice, cheerily hailed. 'Hello!', waved. No good.

Willy scraped his thumb along his wiry beard. A static

171

crackle, like a premonition of lightning, sparked along his jaw. 'When my son, Samuel, has acted unwisely,' he advised, 'I encourage him to speak. I assure him that confession is like repeating a dream in the sunshine. He is constantly surprised by the depths of my understanding.'

'There's nothing to confess,' Letherbridge muttered. 'That's the horrible thing. I don't know what happened.'

18

It had all been arranged, he told us. Charlie had been paid; the party was to take place; the girl had been invited. Letherbridge's henchmen were going too and, like me, they decided to follow Karen, Linda from her point of departure.

They rang the same doorbell I was later to ring and the same landlord answered it. On the doorstep he tried to sell them a bundle of old magazines. Some of the pages were missing and some were stuck together. They bought them, though, because they realised they were the admission fee, and threw them into the road. 'The girl,' they said. 'We've come to wait for the girl.'

'Come inside, boys. Come inside,' the landlord said. He retreated, sideways, in front of them, beckoning them into a room off the hallway. Then he shoved his face close to theirs. His breath smelt of sardines. He whispered, 'She usually goes out about now. If you go upstairs and peep through the keyhole you can see her getting dressed. For a consideration, boys. For a consideration.' He clacked his false teeth at them and held out a yellowed claw. 'You can see everything,' he whined. 'Tits. I bet you boys would like to see tits, eh?' He poked one of them in the chest.

They declined his offer. They chose to wait until the girl left the house, the landlord hopping around them all the time, itemising her anatomy. When she went out, they followed her.

The last description I have of her, consequently, is theirs – and even that came struggling through Letherbridge's cloudy, bitter mind. He reminded me of a drunk in a café, reminiscing till dawn about a scheme or a love that had failed him. It wasn't his fault, of course. His voice became fuzzy and muffled, like a record played by a dusty stylus. His fleshy hands loosened and his ball-bearing dropped to the carpet. It bounced once, and settled by the railway line.

And, behind his henchboys, I shadowed the girl – what was her name, anyway? – glimpsing bits of her between those doubled shoulders. Black, white collar backs, upright like door-to-door missionaries. They had dressed with colonial rectitude on that dry Saturday evening, as if in severe distinction from their quarry.

Her platinum hair lined stiffly down to a leather jacket. Steely hair against calf-caramel brown, so that her clothing seemed more animal than she. A soft skirt jerked whitely, as though invisible fingers tugged at its hem, with each step. Her walk jolted her forward on high heels. She wore a fragile chain around one ankle.

She was taller and thinner than in my previous fantasies, as if her infringement on reality had begun to extrude her lengthwise. I wondered what it would be like to fuck her. I thought of the skeleton prominent beneath the skin. The base of a cup grinding on a saucer. A sexual act with a girl who was, after all, dead. Enough.

They – the henchboys – said she went to a pub. She sat on a bar stool, legs folded together like an emaciated mermaid's tail. She drank with repetitive swiftness, elbow out wide and wrist tipping the glass until it tapped the bridge of her nose. Nicola – to quote Letherbridge – 'came in and picked her up.'

The boys followed them from pub to party. They watched them go into the block of flats, vanishing in the doorway behind a rectangular sheet of light. Remaining themselves on the pavement, I thought I detected a shuffling what-do-we-do-nowness in their posture, a faltering. And then I realised they were waiting for an opportunity to slip in unobserved and soon I saw their opportunity – in the shape of Eth and me – coming down the street.

Eth, next to me on the sofa, winced away. But, that night, we had been comrades-in-arms, staggering together; and the henchboys had worn us like a mask, their plain faces behind our gaudy entrance. There were some ragged cries . . .

'And, during the party,' Letherbridge concluded, 'the murder was committed.'

'During the party the murder was committed!' I repeated incredulously. 'How? You can't just leave it there.'

'But I have to.' He gave a weak, inadequate shrug. 'My boys saw nothing. There was no disturbance. She was there, then she was gone. Your friend Charlie – he killed her by sleight of hand.'

We could hear a lavatory being flushed over and over again upstairs.

'Mr Letherbridge,' said Willy, 'at the commencement of our conversation you suggested that we should ask you questions – that we should attempt to verify. Your story is consistent with what we know, but still I do not believe it. How do you propose to convince me?'

We could hear the vacuum cleaner coming down the staircase. The stifled suck on a strip of carpet, a whistling gulp in the air, and then the suck again. A lateral foot stepping down after it.

'I haven't got long,' Letherbridge whined, like a senile

vampire about to crumble into dust. He got down on all fours and began worriedly to disconnect two lengths of track. The tip of his tongue bitten between his teeth.

Eth suddenly swooped from the sofa – a swift, curving movement, descending on his silver ball. She beaked it in finger and thumb, and stood perched on the carpet as though it were a lofty branch.

He looked up at her, his eyes wide and watery. 'Give it to me,' he pleaded. 'It's my – my thing.' It was how I imagined a labrador would talk, if it could.

'You're a liar.'

'There are many ways, Mr Letherbridge, of extracting the truth. A confession is by far the easiest,' Willy warned him.

'Give me my ball back.'

'No.' Eth clutching it tight.

'Look – ' I began. The situation struck me as more than faintly ridiculous. We were deadlocked over a pair of incommensurable quantities – Eth with a ball-bearing; Letherbridge, perhaps, with some residual portion of the truth – and neither likely to be relinquished for the other. Meanwhile, Willy was hinting that a little judicious torture might resolve the impasse. I was searching desperately for a compromise.

Letherbridge trundled over to the sideboard. He pulled six shoe boxes from under it and, with his left hand, began piling strips of railway line into one of them. His right hand danced solitary on the floor.

Coming down the hallway – which ran, I supposed, from the front door to the kitchen – were the short punctilious strokes of a brush. The sweep towards the dustpan and a face hanging over it. The creeping wife.

'I'm going to kick this engine,' Eth announced. Her toe measured a short arc to an earthbound locomotive, intimating a point of contact dead centre.

Letherbridge babooned across the room and snatched his toy from peril, his lower jaw caught in a convulsive gibber.

'Or this one,' said Eth, and stepped over to a blue and gold diesel.

The brush was proceeding down the corridor towards us.

'The diary!' I remembered blindingly. 'Give us the diary and we'll go.' If there was corroboration to be found, it had to be there.

'My daughter's . . .' he muttered ' . . . relic.'

'You want your ball back, don't you? Come on, man!'

'In that drawer.' He pointed.

Eth, not for the first time, put her foot down. I went over to the sideboard, opened the drawer indicated and rummaged inside. Down past the folded napkins, beneath a set of table mats depicting scenes from the Lake District, I rooted out a shabby exercise book covered in Christmas wrapping paper.

'This?' I asked. He nodded.

'It is sufficient,' said Willy. 'We shall go.'

'Let me look at it,' Eth demanded. She stood with both hands outstretched, the ball balanced on one palm, the other empty. It was a monumental pose, like an allegorical statue. But an allegory for what?

As I passed the diary to her, she tipped Letherbridge's fetish slowly to the carpet. He made a grateful grab for it. Eth started turning the pages of his daughter's record. I could hear the brush tickling the door, as close as a moustache to a lip.

Willy drew the curtains back across the patio window. An iceberg of light, dissolving, floated into the room. His blunt fingers pushed the catch up on the frame. He heaved his bulk against it and the window rolled aside. Air came oozing in. Daytime.

'Mr Paris,' said Willy, 'we shall leave this way.'

'Worthless!' Eth shrieked. 'Cheated!' Her eyes, blank with scandal, fixed on the diary's cover where a reindeer whisked its sleigh over red rooftops. 'Worthless!' she repeated, and delivered a series of straight-legged kicks to tracks, trains, signals and sidings. Letherbridge scuttled this way and that, catching his broken toys, his twisted rails, as they shot from wall to wall, scrabbling for springs and tiny nuts and bolts.

Willy seized her by the elbows and dragged her out through the open window, across the patio and on to the lawn beyond; me following. We stopped, all breathless. I glanced back to the house to see Letherbridge kneeling, visible between the curtains. He was pale like limestone in the morning light, shadows like cracks in the folds of his dressing gown, clasping a locomotive to his beating heart.

Eth shook Willy off. 'It's all right,' she told him. 'I can walk.' And promptly stumbled, her heel miraculously embedded in a papier-mâché hill.

Eth sat in the back of the car, silent, her anger as palpable as a cold hand on my neck. I think she felt that Willy and I had let her down. We had declined to be violent when the moment for violence came. We had succumbed too easily to deceit and obfuscation; wound round us like string, till we were tied in the knot of narrative.

I flicked idly through the diary, digesting disgust at my own gullibility. It was similar to discovering that an expensive-looking watch, bought from a street trader, was a cheap fraud. I should have known it would be.

'Hurray! Did it for the first time tonight. Daddy seemed surprised . . . And again (twice!) . . . Persuaded him to go on top. Not sure whether I like this as much . . . Told me that I was a lot younger than Mummy, which I knew anyway . . . Got nasty tonight because I said I couldn't. Men! . . . Drempt [sic] about Dave. Do I love him? Maybe . . . Daddy is becoming a pest. I decided to lock my bedroom door . . . He has taken the key away. Oh well! . . .'

And so it went on, three dated years of it, right to the final twists of leaving home. Naïve, authentic phrases – and every line in Letherbridge's handwriting.

'It's impenetrable!' Eth suddenly burst out. Her fist smote the back of my seat. The cushioned leather sighed back into place. 'It's lies, lies, impenetrable lies!'

'Young lady,' said Willy, half turning, one eye on the ribboning road, 'you will please show greater respect for my property.'

The silence resumed. It was like having a fourth presence sulking in our midst. We drove through the suburbs and I stared out at the kisses snatched across a briefcase, the goodbyes waved from a doorstep, with the feeling that I was reviewing a fictional orderliness – a mime by an accomplished troupe. The traffic was becoming more dense and the little bodies hurtled on the pavement more frantically the nearer we approached to the city. It could have been they were desperate to convince me, to charm me out of my dislocation.

Last night had had the effect of a display of magic on me; one wizardry merging into another, cards shuffled, illusion dissolving into illusion. I had stepped out of the common run of things and glimpsed an extraordinary otherness; and now I had to step back. But, in memory's vivid cinema, those disconcerting realities played for me again. What I had seen had happened. I was sure I was doomed to be a heretic against life.

We dropped Eth off first. Standing outside the car, she seemed to loom larger – as though she had been compressed or folded before. She knocked on my window and I rolled it down.

'You gave up,' she accused. 'You could have had him and you let him go. You let him fool you.'

Willy drummed the steering wheel, tapping out the rhythm of his impatience, eager to be gone.

'Have you given up?' I asked her. I knew that, whatever her reply, I was bound to be upset by it.

'Wait,' she ordered.

Timorously, I watched her unlocking her front door – its white-diamond panels with their fairytale freshness – and closing it after her. We waited obediently, scanning her flat's impassive countenance, and soon a window twitched and opened like a waking eye. Eth was standing inside – her throat arched, her head thrown back, her whole body apparently attuned to an inarticulate cry and her legendary red hair flowing out like a train behind it – balancing a cardboard box on the sill. And, with a stiff-elbowed action, she took a bottle from the box and flung it into the street. And another and another followed it – all the bottles I had emptied in my sojourn there – until the pavement glittered with a silver spray.

We drove off, having witnessed her way of saying goodbye. The vandalism of the heart, I supposed. It was as if those bottles represented – what? Sins, omissions, things not done or done without commitment. The loud and glorious symbol that her hopes for me were truly at an end.

'Now you will understand,' said Willy, 'why I have concealed things from her.'

'Whuh,' I murmured. I had been sinking down the long, grey funnel of sleep, bidding adieu to wisps of our adventure as they sailed smokily by. Willy's lullaby tones seemed half to belong to my half-dream.

'Outrage, anger, the urge to do violence – these emotions should be deployed with care. We should invest them where they are most profitable to us. They should not be entrusted to women.'

'Uh huh.'

'Mr Paris, pay attention to me. Perhaps I have not so much concealed things from her as declined to draw her attention to certain features of the case.'

'Whah?'

'For example, why should a man steal a diary if he himself had forged it?'

'Pardon?' My neck wrenched itself as if I had been woken up by a noose. A brutal jerk to consciousness.

'You will recall that your Mr Letherbridge applied cigars to the girl Nina's foot in order to obtain' – left hand seizing the exercise book from the dashboard and shaking it by the spine – 'this. The girl Karen had been in possession of it. She attempted to hide it from him. Does that suggest to you a worthless forgery?'

'No. But – '

'The handwriting? You have made an incorrect assumption.'

'Come on,' I protested. 'It's identical to the dedication in the Bible.'

'Exactly so. And who wrote that, Mr Paris?'

'He did. He admitted it himself.'

'No!' He banged the steering wheel and accidentally sounded the horn. His car honkingly signalled agreement with him. 'He admitted only that he recognised the handwriting. It was yourself and Miss Spurgeon who decided – by a process of psychological deduction, performed in a pub – that it was his.'

I was quiet whilst this diagnosis settled like a surprising precipitation of soot, leaving me besmirched and somewhat foolish. 'Then whose was it?'

'His daughter's. It is the true account.'

'So what are we going to do?'

'You will go home and sleep. I have business to conduct with your friend Charlie.'

'What are you going to do to him?' I asked.

'He killed my property.' It sounded like the first proposition of a syllogism. I could guess the middle term and its conclusion.

'Are you going to torture him?'

'The truth, Mr Paris, is like a splinter buried deep beneath the skin. Sometimes it has to be coaxed out with much discomfort; but the end is satisfying to both patient and surgeon.'

'That means "Yes"?'

'Mr Paris,' warned Willy, 'I advise you to sleep long and hard.'

19

In my familiar, unpretentious flat there were signs of
builders: cement dust footprints up the staircase; a trowel, a
few loose bricks and a yellow bucket in the kitchen; a couple
of powdery sacks, also, like fat and scowling gnomes. The
hole had diminished to a disappointing tidiness.

And there was a note from my landlord:

> Dear Mr Paris,
>   It should not be necessary for me to point out that
> the causing of explosions is in breach of our tenancy
> agreement. Quite apart from other considerations, your
> flying bath might easily have killed innocent children. I
> must therefore insist that you seek accommodation more
> suitable to your present lifestyle.

Fuck him, I thought. Fuck the innocent children too,
come to that.

I decided to lie down, and meandered through to the
bedroom, where so much of my lifestyle was located. I
stretched out on the mattress and reflected that, really, this
was a moment for personal heroism. Call a cab. Dash across
London. Rescue Charlie from the fate impending. Make
our escape seconds before Willy and his goons – equipped
with razors, switchblades, hammers and other surgical
instruments – embraced him with their retributive care.

I wondered how Charlie would stand up to torture;
whether he would think of something witty to say – a
defiant one-liner, of the sort Catholic martyrs habitually
managed. 'If I had served my friends as I have served my
nose . . .'

'Bastard!'

'I'm sorry?' I found myself addressing the floor, whence this remark seemed to issue.

An elbow, clad in black velvet, protruded from under the bed, then a green-corduroyed knee. A shoulder and a foot followed and my bed's springs agitatedly groaned, as if they were giving birth to a wastrel, fully formed.

'Charles! My son!'

'Angelo, my child. You were squashing me.'

'What are you doing here?'

'Hiding.' He picked a flake of rust out of his hair and dropped it with distaste, like a flea. 'I was afraid you'd brought that black bugger back with you. I saw his car outside.'

'But how did you know to hide?'

'Angelo, Angelo.' A sad shake of the head. 'I keep telling you you're not very bright – and you never believe me. Nicola warned me that you and Eth had visited her so I guessed it was probable you would get round to visiting Letherbridge. And knowing him as I do, I thought it was likely he would give me away.'

'And Letherbridge?' I enquired. 'Had he been warned as well?'

'Oh yes. We've been in contact all along. Funny man. Bit of an eccentric.'

'I'd noticed.'

'Do you know, when I told him you might be on your way, his only reaction was to mutter something about having to go to Hamleys?'

'I can believe it,' I assured him bitterly.

Charlie arranged himself in my deckchair. He was the only person I've ever met who could give an appearance of being comfortable in it. Perhaps the skin and bone structure of his body had a peculiar affinity with canvas and sticks.

I regretted my regret at the prospect of his being tortured. It seemed reasonable, just then, to assume that a good dose of agony would be positively healthy for him. He, after all, was responsible more than anyone for the torments I had suffered. He reminded me of some mischievous and elegant sprite, choosing to appear to me now primarily out of vanity. He was enjoying recounting how I had been fooled.

'How did you kill her?' I asked.

'I didn't. I only arranged things. I wanted it to go off smoothly – so as not to interfere with the party.'

The girl had been alone beside the drinks table, and Charlie had watched her across the peopled room – planetary dancers revolving to obscure her, like the slow periods of darkness that a lighthouse leaves. He had enticed her there because Nicola was guilty.

'Guilty,' he explained, 'about having sold her to Willy. So I persuaded her to find Karen and bring her to the party. And I promised that I would introduce her to a nice young man who would look after her. Protect her from the pimps.'

I saw Charlie slouching against the wall, devising a Renaissance disaster; and Mick, with crooked knee, arriving at his side, importunately attending trouble's indifferent form. Piratically he spied out the land as Charlie murmured –

'I think it should be done.'

'You want me to do a little damage? To teach her what a woman's really for?'

'I think you should take it further than that,' said Charlie, nodding his head in contemplative self-agreement. 'The back room's empty. The one where Nicola used to keep her bike.'

'You want me to give her a fucking good hiding? Turn her fucking arse red?'

'No,' said Charlie. 'A little further than that.'

Mick set down his drink and took his way obliquely through the dancers. Charlie regarded him like a clockmaker who had set an uncertain instrument into motion. This was the first, experimental winding up.

Mick uncoiled to Karen's side – each pace a calibration to

the moment when her death was due. A jellied squint was squirming in his eyes, as if one of them was attached to a trembling spring.

'But why didn't she resist?' I demanded.

'Because she was a prostitute. You see, Angelo, out in the big, wide world, there are men who get their kicks in strange ways. I told the girl I had a friend who was, *inter alia*, a sadist and asked if she would be kind enough to take care of his needs. She agreed. I paid her. And all the time Mick was doing the business, she thought he was simply having fun.'

Then he began to laugh. The same rippling, brook-bubbling laugh I had heard in his flat that sunny Sunday morning long ago.

'I'm sorry,' I interrupted pompously, 'I don't see the joke.'

'Well, the funny thing is,' he looked up at me, the palms of his hands flattened against his face to smooth away the rictus of hysteria, 'that when Nicola saw how ugly Mick was she swore Karen wouldn't have anything to do with him. So I had a side bet with her that they would be lovers before the night was out. And when Mick was sorting her out I took Nicola to the door of the back room to listen. And she listened to the grunts and the cries and the squeals' he spluttered, 'and turned round and paid me.'

In a few hours my flat will be repaired, and that will be the end of the only sign that anything was ever disturbed. I shall be immured – until such time as my landlord carries out his threat to evict me – in peace again with my deckchair, my poster of Debbie Harry, my Marmite. Even my spider, or one indistinguishable from it, has returned to travel up and down on its invisible thread.

Yesterday, as if to indicate that it was over for him too, Willy paid me a visit. The builders had left the front door open, so he was able, without preliminary negotiations, to install himself before me. I was lying on my bed thinking of the many theatre companies I could write to for a part, the many replies I would never receive – so that my life stretched out measurably in terms of letters that wouldn't come – the cigarettes I would smoke without being aware that I'd lit them, the cups of coffee that would sluice through me.

And thinking also of Eth, whom I would betray by never telling her any of what I knew. Henceforth, I would be completely safe from her. A constant peril, a tormentor, a crude conscience shouting in one ear was out of my life. Hooray. A flat cheer for Eth's future absence. She was one of those people – like the bullying sergeant-major or the tyrannical schoolmaster – whom you suspect you will eventually come to think of as having been good for you.

And of Charlie, who had borrowed seventeen pounds from me in order to flee to Stoke Poges – where, he claimed, he had a brother in the arms trade.

Then I looked up and saw Willy standing there, solemn as a priest.

'You live here,' he said.

'Yes,' I confessed. I gestured decadently. 'All this is mine.'

He was wearing a camel-brown overcoat and a burgundy scarf tucked, cravat-style, at his neck. The plumb-line creases in his trousers descended exactly to the centre of his shoes.

'I shall sit,' he announced. And did so, guiding himself down to the deckchair as if he were a load being lowered from a crane. He attempted to cross his legs, but the deckchair's subversive frame threatened to unseat him. He removed his hat instead, placed it on the floor and patted it.

'I have been unable to locate your friend Charlie,' he mourned. 'Therefore I cannot describe to you the mechanism of the murder. I can, however, satisfy your curiosity on another matter.'

'The dedication?' I speculated. 'What it meant? Why she wrote it?'

'That also, if you wish.'

'What else is there?'

'The grave, Mr Paris. Are you not curious about that?'

'No,' I told him. 'Why should I be?'

'It was an extraordinary grave. But I shall tell you about the dedication first. It is from the story of Jephthah – an unfortunate man who made a bargain with his God. He vowed that, if he was granted victory in battle, he would sacrifice the first beast that met him when he returned home. Doubtless he expected a sheep or a goat; but it was his daughter whom he encountered.

'Father and daughter agreed to keep the vow. Thereafter, however, the narrative becomes obscure. It relates that the girl requested "let me alone for two months, that I may go up and down upon the mountains, and bewail my virginity, I and my fellows." '

'The Bible tells us very little more; only that "she returned unto her father, who did with her according to his vow which he had vowed." The story is concluded enigmatically; its emphasis, it seems to me, is not upon death.'

'And the grave?' I said. 'Why is that extraordinary?'

'Ah. Mr Paris, you must understand that there are two sorts of grave. There are those which are monuments, and there are those which are places of concealment. When I first saw the girl's, I asked myself which type it was.'

'A place of concealment,' I suggested.

'So it would seem. But was it not, Mr Paris, a very obvious grave? A mound at the bottom of a garden, covered with a scattering of leaves; is this not – I repeat the word – obvious? Is this not exactly what you would have expected to find?'

'Yes,' I protested. 'But surely – '

Willy held up his hand. 'A man may dig a grave to hide a body. Or he may – and this is a darker crime – dig a grave because he wishes to pretend that a body is hidden.'

'I don't see – '

186

'Mr Paris, what did you find in the grave?'

'Nothing,' I replied. 'A tree root.'

'This is correct,' said Willy. 'Nothing and a tree root.'

'I don't see – ' I protested again.

And Willy interrupted me for the second time. 'Precisely. You do not see. You have not seen those things which you ought to have seen and you have imagined things which you did not see at all. You have not, for example, seen a body; and yet you remain convinced that there was a murder.'

'But I saw!' I insisted. 'I saw her in the room after the party.'

'I suspect that you saw a girl who had been badly beaten up. Perhaps your friend Charlie, who is a specialist in narcotics, had administered some additional substance to her. I believe that you saw all these things. But I do not think you saw a corpse.'

'Then where is she?' I demanded. 'The girl – what's become of her?'

'Mr Paris, do you not feel – in your heart of hearts – that what we witnessed the other night was – how shall I say? – a feast of delusion?' His hands mimed a tablecloth across his knees. 'Do you not feel it had all been prepared for us? It is my convinction that your Mr Letherbridge had anticipated our arrival.'

'Quite possibly,' I concurred. 'So what?'

'It is the technique of magicians to distract the attention whilst the real business is carried on out of sight. This magician amused us with his confession to murder in order to conceal the fact that the girl was still alive. I believe your friend Charlie was paid not to kill her but to return her, chastened, to her father. I cannot be sure, though, since your friend has escaped me. And, even if I had found him, would he have told me the truth?'

'Who knows?' I said. 'It's a tricky question.'

Willy pondered for a moment. Perhaps he had never encountered the dilemma of uncertainty before. Then he said, 'There are crimes worse than murder. The procurement of a resurrection may be one. Your Mr Letherbridge was a religious man; he made a monument of an empty grave. The parallel would not have eluded him.'

After that, we talked. But it was no more than a necessary epilogue. We were searching for a way of saying goodbye to each other – a diplomatic formula which would concede respect on both sides.

'People will always distrust you,' I told him. 'They'll always think you know too much.'

It was the best I could manage and, naturally, I expected him to go one better.

He picked up his hat and peered into its depth. He frowned, so that his brow creased into scrolled folds.

'When my son, Samuel, is older,' he declared, 'I hope he will have your. . .' He halted, faltered, and stared more penetratingly into his hat as though the vanished word had once been written there. Then he began afresh.

'Next time we are reading a play together,' he promised, 'I shall tell him that I once knew an actor.'